WHEN TOYS WERE FUN

Revisit the Happy Days of Childhood Collecting

BRYAN APPS

HALSGROVE

To my grandchildren,
Kieren, Katelin and Lucy

First published in Great Britain in 2010

Copyright © Bryan Apps 2010

British Library Cataloguing-in-Publication Data
A CIP record for this title is available from the British Library

ISBN 978 0 85704 040 4

HALSGROVE
Halsgrove House,
Ryelands Industrial Estate,
Bagley Road, Wellington, Somerset TA21 9PZ
Tel: 01823 653777   Fax: 01823 216796
email: sales@halsgrove.com

Part of the Halsgrove group of companies
Information on all Halsgrove titles is available at: www.halsgrove.com

Printed and bound in China by Toppan Leefung Printing Ltd

CONTENTS

Bibliography & Acknowledgements

The Art of the Tin Toy by David Pressland, *A Century of Model Trains* by Allen Levy, *L'age d'or des Jouets* by J. Remise and J. Fondin, *The Great Toys of George Carette* New Cavendish Press, *Toy Boats* by Jacques Milet and Robert Forbes, *Great Toys – Marklin 1895 – 1914* Denys Ingram, *History of British Dinky Toys 1934 – 1964* by Cecil Gibson, *Clockwork, Steam and Electric – The History of Model Railways up to 1939.* By Gustav Reder, *Toy Cars* by Gordon Gardiner and Richard O'Neill, *Toy Autos 1890 – 1939 The Peter Ottenheimer Collection* Victor Gollancz Ltd. *The Hornby Book of Trains, The Tri-ang Book of Trains. Bassett-Lowke Railways, The History of Toys* by Deborah Jaffe.

In the compilation of this book thanks are due to Hornby Hobbies, Harrods, Hamleys, National Motor Museum, Renown Pictures Ltd, Solent News Agency, Southern Daily Echo, P.G. Wright, D.R. Apps, E. Gee, and my wife Kath for her support and encouragement.

'King George II' at Dawlish in 1938.

1
WHEN TOYS WERE FUN

O LEVELS WERE ONLY WEEKS AWAY, and we had been told that we could take the afternoon off from school. Alistair Sim was in 'Scrooge' at the Odeon and this seemed to offer an entertaining way to brush up on my English Literature. As I sat in the darkness, amidst rows of largely empty seats, I became totally absorbed in the film of that familiar story by Charles Dickens. But what impressed me more than the old miser and the Ghosts of Christmas was the scene in which Tiny Tim gazed through a shop window at a display of Victorian toys. There were automata performing lifelike actions and, in the foreground, a jolly fat man with a top hat rocked to and fro with laughter. Another figure with the face of a monkey played a harp, but my attention was drawn to a superb model of a paddle steamer with a tall funnel, and large splashers to protect its diminutive lead passengers from the spray. Could it have been made by one of the famous toy makers of Nuremberg over a hundred years ago? Tiny Tim gazed at the toy with wonder and delight, and I shared his disappointment when the boat was removed from the window to be sold to a wealthy customer. Clearly, nothing remotely like that paddle steamer would come his way or mine that Christmas.

Tiny Tim gazing at the toy paddle steamer.
Courtesy Renown Pictures Ltd

Was the paddle steamer a toy or a model? It was both, and this is the case with most of the objects which are the subject of this book.

Toys and models

At what point does a train set become a model railway, and at what stage in his life does a young railway enthusiast begin to deny that he is merely 'playing trains'? These are questions which are impossible to answer and I like the sentiment which was inscribed above the door to the room in which Liberace displayed his collection of miniature pianos: "The difference between men and boys is the price they pay for their toys." There is a sense in which the most accurate scale model of a car, boat or train is no more than a very expensive toy, and might it not also be said that Sunseeker yachts and Ferrari sports cars are no more than the playthings of the rich? That, at any rate, is my excuse for including in this volume some of what I consider to be the finest models ever made. On the other hand, I have not included such items as the 'India rubber ball' which A. A. Milne's King John wanted Father Christmas to bring him on 25 December, because a ball is not a very interesting object, unless it happens to be the one used in the Final of the 1966 World Cup. Dolls, doll's houses and doll's prams will be found, as is only right, but I freely admit that there are many more images in this book of boys' toys, most of which happen to run on wheels. This isn't because I subscribe to the adage that boys play with their toys while girls talk to their mothers, but because I believe that the peculiar relationship boys have with their toys is a more lasting one than that of girls with their dolls. Generally I find that girls are more ready to put away childish things than boys whereas, to coin a phrase, you can never entirely take the boy out of the man. Ask

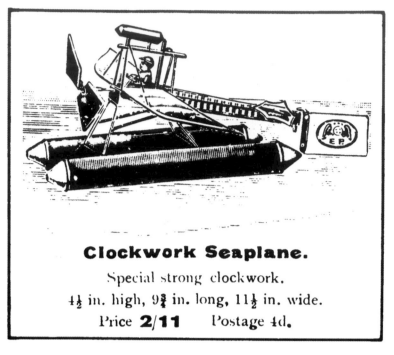

Clockwork Seaplane.

Special strong clockwork.
4½ in. high, 9¾ in. long, 11½ in. wide.
Price **2/11**   Postage 4d.

Mechanical Railway Porter.

An exceedingly clever Toy, with most lifelike movement. The man bends his knees and walks by mechanism contained in his body. Price **1/3** post 3d.

Clockwork Swimming Lady (as illustration). This is **one** of the most realistic Swimming Toys imaginable, it represents a girl in silk costume swimming the breast stroke, and propelled solely **by** the action of the legs and arms. Does not easily get out of order.
Price ..   ..   .. **6/11**   Post 3d.

Supplied in G.W.R., M.R., L. & N.W.R., Lancashire and Yorkshire Railway colours.

Toy or model? Gauge III Bing
'King Edward'.

your wife it you don't believe me! For this reason I unashamedly present a preponderance of toy cars, boats and trains in this book for the particular enjoyment of boys and men of all ages. For so many of us our interest in such things has amounted to an obsession, and it is an obsession which, within the pages of this book, I have indulged. *When Toys Were Fun* is not an encyclopaedia which attempts to cover every toy and model that has ever been made, but is instead a personal view of enjoying and collecting.

A gift for my grandson

When my grandson was eight years old I bought him a toy car as an extra birthday present. It was a diecast model with doors that could be opened, tyres that had treads, and seats with simulated leather upholstery. It was presented in a colourful cardboard box with a 'window' in the front through which it could be viewed and, in spite of being comparatively inexpensive, it was a remarkably accurate representation of its full-scale counterpart. Now my grandson is a good-hearted soul and doesn't have an ungrateful bone in his body, but when he saw what was inside Tesco's finest birthday wrapping paper, he put it to one side unopened, and went back his computer game. It made me reflect upon the fact that when I was his age such a toy would have commanded all of my attention. So what has happened in the intervening years to effect such a change?

Definitions

My dictionary tells me that a toy is 'an object designed to be played with which is a non-functioning replica of something else'. That is not an exhaustive definition but, for generations of children, going back before the beginning of the twentieth century, toy cars, boats and trains were precisely that, except that many of them functioned, being powered by clockwork, electricity or steam. Essentially, they were

A man and a boy with their trains.

objects to handle and enjoy, possess and treasure. But, in the years that have elapsed since my childhood, a great technological revolution has taken place. For most children today what passes for toys are intangible images on video screens which can only be manipulated remotely through a hand control. These twenty-first century toys have to do with what is called virtual reality, which is not in fact reality at all. Through their video games young people can move images around which possess no more than the appearance of being solid objects. Their operators can make them do whatever they want of them, and often end up simulating their destruction with either a crash or an explosion. Well, what else are they expected to do with them? I recognise that video games require skill and dexterity and can be great fun, but I wonder if children today are ever oppressed by a sense of unreality. If I gave reign to the grumpy old man that lurks inside me I might find myself wondering whether these children will prefer in later life to enjoy their foreign holidays without actually moving from their homes and simply by sitting in front of their screens! In addition to computer games, television programmes and DVDs also absorb the attention of children today so that many of them may have little time or inclination to play with real toys. Yet toys are not just for fun they can be educative too, engaging the mind and imagination of children in a way that is much more healthy and constructive than many of the images which they put through their paces on screens.

Opposite: Early mechanical toys advertised in a Gamages catalogue dated 1913.

Gauge OO—⅝ in.

'Hands on' toys for all ages.

Fun

Fun is a word that also needs to be defined. There is fun to be had in taking one's pleasures seriously whether it concerns, for example, golf or model railways. So, in order to treat my subject with sufficient seriousness, I must frequently refer to the gauges of model trains and the reader needs to know what this means. Gauges represent the distance between the rails and, consequently the scale of the model. Gauge IV = 3 inches, gauge III = 2½ inches, 0 gauge = 1¼ inches and 00 = 0.625 inches. The accompanying photograph below shows model engines of the three smaller gauges and from it one can estimate the size of gauge II, III and IV models. In the case of L.G.B garden railways the Swiss and Austrian trains are built to a narrow gauge, like 'the little trains of Wales' so while their rails are 2.5 inches apart their actual scale is greater than gauge III.

This book is about a time when toys were fun because they could be both seen and handled. They were valued all the more in families where money was scarce and at times when the toy manufacturers had to divert their resources from making toys to producing the weapons of war. For me it is especially about a time when children wrote their letters to Father Christmas and sent them up their chimneys in a draught of hot air from open coal fires, in the hope that just one or two items in their wish lists might appear at the foot of their beds when they woke up on Christmas morning.

In sharp contrast, today many children submit their orders well before Christmas as a matter of course, and woe betide their parents if just one of the items is found to be missing! I don't argue in this book that toys and models are no longer fun, or that there is any shortage of them. I only contend that most children above a certain age no longer seem to enjoy them as their fathers once did.

Collecting early toys

A major part this book is about the toys I once owned but own no more. The truth is that I had to part with my collection for a number of reasons, not least of which was the impossibility of accommodating it within a house of modest size when I retired. But collecting early toys and models was enormous fun and, on those rare occasions when I chanced upon items which had only previously been known to collectors through illustrations in early catalogues, a source of great joy.

Gauges I, 0 and 00.

If anyone was to ask me how he should go about collecting antique toys I would advise him to go back to 1960 and to start from then! The reason for this is because in those days it hadn't yet occurred to many people that toys and models were desirable objects for anyone to collect, and the result was that they were relatively inexpensive and easy to find. What was invaluable, in enabling me to recognise the make, date and value of the early toys, were the original catalogues of Gamages, Carette, Bassett-Lowke and Hornby which it was still possible to obtain, and richly illustrated books such as *The Art of the Tin Toy* by David Pressland, and *A History of Model Trains* by Allan Levy. The next best thing to owning a rare toy is to possess a photograph of it and so, in addition to photographs of some of the toys that I collected in the 60s and 70s, I have also included in this book, with the help of Hornby Hobbies, Harrods and Hamleys, many images from the early catalogues of Hornby, Tri-ang, Minic, Scalextric, and others.

Crescent Racing Cars

The process by which I became a toy collector was quite unpremeditated. It came about through going to a café off the Banbury Road for a cup of coffee one morning in 1960 when I was at Oxford. This involved passing a sub post office and I was stopped in my tracks when I spotted a 1:43 scale toy Cooper Bristol in its window. Having witnessed Mike Hawthorn's meteoric rise to fame in his unpainted Cooper Bristol at Goodwood in 1952, I went into the shop to examine the toy at close quarters. I discovered that it was made by Crescent Toys and I judged it to be a far more accurate model of the car than the one made by Dinky Toys at the time. I wondered why the Crescent toy was not better known and could only put it down to the lurid colours of its box and its naive racing numbers, both of which made it superficially less attractive than the product of its better known rival. Perhaps it was simply that

BRM. and Cooper-Bristol Crescent racing cars

it was hard for Crescent Toys to make an impact on a market which Dinky Toys and Corgi had made their own. I was determined to track down whatever other racing cars were made by Crescent Toys and began to search the small corner shops as the ones most likely to stock such an inexpensive toy. Grown men didn't collect toy cars in those days so I felt a little self conscious and talked loudly about my young nephew who would have a birthday soon. Before long a pale blue Gordini came to light which was every bit as good as the Cooper Bristol, and a model that Dinky Toys had overlooked. Then I came across a Crescent V16 BRM. It was the wrong colour green and had a Mark I tail attached to a Mark II body but, even so, it was an excellent model which no one else had thought of making. Over a period of several months I was able to add to my collection of Crescent racing cars a 250F Maserati, a Ferrari 500, an Aston Martin DB3S, an A Type Connaught and a Vanwall. All of these more than lived up to my expectations following the discovery of the original Cooper Bristol. After this I could find no more and, strangely, never came upon a dupli-

Gordini and Connaught Crescent racing cars

cate of any of the toys I already possessed. I wrote to Crescent Toys in Cardiff to ask for help and they confirmed what I had suspected. They had discontinued the manufacture of their range of racing cars, but the good news was that they sent me the last two toys on their shelves. One was a W196 Mercedes Benz and the other a D Type Jaguar, and the amazing thing was that they were only two models in their range that were missing from my collection! Crescent also sent me the remainder of their stock of racing car numbers in clearing their shelves of anything to do with their toy cars. So it was in this way that I stumbled into becoming a collector, but I committed the heinous sin of carefully repainting each car and replacing the number transfers with ones which looked more authentic. I even modified the tail of the BRM so that it matched the rest of the car. I also added to my small collection two Dinky Toys, a 158 Alfa Romeo and a Lago Talbot, and made a glass-fronted wooden case in which to display them. Crescent racing cars have since become favourites with many collectors but their base plates are sometimes subject to metal fatigue which causes them to become soft and crumble.

A Lesney Yesteryear Ford T

A few years later, when I was married and had a small son, I resumed the hobby of collecting toy cars, again more by accident than design. My son Richard had woken up with a high temperature and I decided to buy him a toy to cheer him up. Once more it was in a small corner shop that I

Lesney Yesteryear models. *From front left and from left to right:* Y5 2nd series 1929 4.5 litre Bentley, Y10 2nd series 1928, Mercedes Benz 36/220, Y16 1st series 1904 Spyker, Y15 1st series 1907 Rolls Royce Silver Ghost, Y8 2nd series 1914 Sunbeam motorcycle, Y6 2nd series Type 35 Bugatti (red), Y6 2nd series Type 35 Bugatti (blue), Y7 2nd series 1913 Mercer (mauve), Y7 2nd series 1913 Mercer (yellow) *Second Row:* Y11 2nd series 1912 Packard, Y9 2nd series 1912 Simplex, Y2 2nd series 1911 Renault, Y7 2nd series 1912 Rolls Royce, Y5 3rd series 1907 Peugeot, Y2 3rd series 1914 Vauxhall, Y1 2nd series 1911 Ford T, Y13 2nd series 1911 Daimler *Third Row:* Y16 3rd series 1928 Mercedes Benz, Y11 3rd series 1938 Lagonda, Y15 3rd series 1930 Packard, Y4 3rd series 1909 Opel, Y8 3rd series 1914 Stutz, Y3 2nd series 1910 Benz, Y10 3rd series 1906 Rolls Royce *Back Row:* Y9 2nd series 1912 Simplex, Y6 3rd series 1913 Cadilac, Y15 2nd series 1911 Maxwell, Y12 2nd series 1909 Thomas Flyabout

chanced upon my purchase. It was of a Lesney Yesteryear Ford T, cherry red in colour, and I was struck by the quality of this inexpensive model. Richard was not at all interested in the car, being less than eighteen months old, and so I decided to put it in a safe place beyond his reach! That was the start of my Lesney Yesteryear collection, and it sent me again to the little corner stores in search of the First Series Yesteryear models which, having been discontinued, were no longer to be found in the larger toy shops. Whenever I did find one it was because it had been left unnoticed at the back of a shelf and this meant that it was marked up at its original price which was less than that of the then current Second Series. The model I had most difficulty in locating was the 1908 Grand Prix Mercedes but I soon discovered that, in addition to the basic range, there were rare colour variations to look out for too. I made some open wall-shelves to display the Yesteryear models in our home.

Early Dinky Toys.
From left to right:
Rolls Royce, Daimler,
Vauxhall, Chrysler Airflow.

Becoming a serious collector of antique toys

My interest in collecting toys and models was further stimulated by a rather strange set of circumstances. Ever since reading a series of articles in *Motor Sport* magazine entitled 'Cars I have owned' I had a yearning to own an old car. A garage in the Portobello Road advertised regularly in *Motor Sport* and a trip to London in 1965 resulted in my purchasing a 1936 Riley Adelphi for £150. The car was mechanically sound and, after having it correctly re-sprayed navy blue and black, and having the chrome renewed on its radiator shell and lamps, it was immaculate. Eventually, though, I had to come to terms with the fact that a more mundane Morris Oxford was a more practical form of transport than the Riley.

A collection of early toys.

As a result of owning the Riley I came across a farmer near Andover who restored vintage cars and had recently been to the South of France and back in a full-scale version of the Second Series Yesteryear 1912 Rolls Royce Silver Ghost. One of his larger cow sheds, suitably fitted out, was bursting with interesting old cars and this gave me the idea of following his example but on a much smaller and more affordable scale by collecting toy cars. I began by collecting pre-1950 Dinky Toys. Now the great thing about collecting early toy cars is that, in addition to resembling the cars they were modelled upon, they were also manufactured at the very same time and this meant even more to me when I moved on from Dinky Toys to collect pre-1914 tinplate toys.

Every collector occasionally finds that he has items which he needs to sell, if only to make room for those he has most recently acquired, and I came across someone who always obliged in this respect. He would lay a blanket across the bonnet of his Hillman Minx and then reverently place all the itemsI had for sale out upon it. After a careful examination of each one he would ask me how much I wanted for them and his response was invariably, "You're pushing me," followed by "That's about how much I would be able to get for them myself, can you accept a little less?" Of course I soon realised that I simply had to suggest a slightly higher price in the first place to obtain the price I wanted in the end!

I always tried to be scrupulously fair in purchasing items for my collection because it was no more than an enjoyable hobby and I had no wish to take advantage of others, and especially of those who had carefully preserved them ever since their childhood. In any case, the inflation of the 1970s resulted in what was an excessively high price to pay for an antique toy one month looking more like a bargain later on in the same year!

The author with his trains.
Courtesy Southern Daily Echo

2
A WARTIME CHILDHOOD

MY EARLIEST RECOLLECTION OF A TOY that I could call my own is of a blue teddy bear. It didn't have a name but, as I can't recall a time when it was not almost entirely threadbare, it must have been my closest companion from the day I was born. Had it been coloured pink and belonged to a girl it might well have remained a treasured possession to this day but, amidst all the changing circumstances of life, I have to confess that my much-loved teddy was somehow allowed to disappear without trace years ago. Surely teddy bears, whether they are blue, pink or brown, will always be loved by small children – at least until they are old enough to have their imagination captivated by the insidious influence of virtual reality games.

I was born in 1937, just two years before the Second World War, and so grew up in those dark days when all the energy and resources of the nation not being applied to meeting the basic necessities of life were directed towards the war effort. A shop in the railway town of Eastleigh which had once sold ice cream remained closed until after the war, and there were faded posters next door to it advertising bananas which would not be in the shops again until peace was restored. Constant air raids and the increasing number of bombed sites around my home made me doubt if peace would ever come. To say that toys were scarce would be an understatement, and no shop today would have the effrontery to offer what often passed for toys then. There was a shop in Winchester High Street called 'The Bazaar' which seemed to sell the only toys which were to be had in the whole of the county of Hampshire and which went like hot cakes the moment they appeared on its shelves. The Bazaar offered extremely crude models such as tanks made of wood thinly-coated in dull paint, and armoured cars composed of plaster that had slender lead wheels which wobbled until they fell off their inadequate axles. These lumps of plaster were heavy and crumbled when dropped. Lead soldiers were flat and unpainted, unlike the rounded and colourful Britains figures from the 1930s. Toy aircraft were made of dull unpainted bakelite and these too were sold out almost as soon as they arrived.

The remnants of my eldest brother's battered toys from before the war added a degree of faded quality to my toy cupboard. For example, there were soldiers with pink faces and khaki uniforms that had their heads attached to their necks by matchsticks after having been worsted in many battles, while the First World War-style toy guns which had fired the broken matchsticks that had done the damage were still in good working order. There was a Rolls Royce armoured car from the Great War which had broken wheels, and an 0 gauge 4-4-0 Bassett-Lowke LMS railway engine which had a dented boiler and lacked both front bogie and tender. A wooden fort had

Wartime deprivation in 1943.

The World's Greatest Toys

We are sorry that we cannot supply these famous toys to-day, but they will be ready for you again after the war. Look out for the good times coming!

HORNBY TRAINS

A Hornby Pullman Train passing under a Gantry Signal.

Meccano Magazine November 1943

survived in remarkably good condition. Essentially a painted wooden box, its walls and keep were stowed away inside, to be assembled by being fitted into slots on the top whenever it was used. It was more medieval than twentieth century in style and this probably accounted for its survival. A collection of farmyard animals and some zoo animals with sections of fencing and cages to contain them, came through all the air raids safely as did also my parents, my brothers and myself.

Dinky Toys after the War

Christmas was a challenging time for the mothers of small children in the mid 1940s and my mother still had to use all her ingenuity in the years immediately after the war to ensure that my brother David and I had a good number of presents to unwrap. To achieve this there were bars of soap, face flannels, toothbrushes and oranges which, as our surrogate Father Christmas, she carefully wrapped up in paper and placed in pillow cases during the night before Christmas. We tried to look surprised and to sound grateful but our disappointment must have been all too obvious when the toiletries were revealed. What we frantically searched for as we waded through the pillow cases, digging deep to try to feel parcels of a promising size and weight, were Dinky Toys, and in a good year two or three of the reissued pre-war models might come to light. One year I had an American Oldsmobile in that odd shade of oily blue, a mid green Lagonda sports car with dark green seats and spare wheel covers on either side of its long bonnet, and a black and maroon London taxi. I remember that my brother David's taxi was black and bright green. We carefully placed our finds side by side, hardly allowing them out of our sight all that day and the next. On Christmas evening, while our parents played Monopoly in the smoke-filled dining room with the Durbans from four doors away, David and I continued to enjoy the Dinky Toys, handling them with infinite care as we admired their shiny new paint. These toys were much more than fun in our eyes. We felt as though we had become men of substance and we revelled in our new-found possessions.

It is worth recording how Father Christmas managed to obtain these rare toys of such superior quality. It involved mother placing an order for them with Bowleys, a toy shop in Market Street Eastleigh, many months before. There was always a long waiting list for Dinky Toys, as there also was for real cars in the years after the war, and the fact that my father owned a men's outfitter's shop opposite the toy shop possibly meant that her order was given a slightly higher priority than some of the others. Even so, the tiny vehicles would become available only one and two at a time during the course of the year and they would be pounced upon by mother as though they were made of pure gold.

They say that familiarity breeds contempt and the converse is also surely true. The extreme shortage of toys during the Second World War eventually gave rise to a generation of adult toy collectors who had been starved of toys when they were young. And when this caused prices to rise, as demand far exceeded supply, manufacturers produced new models of ever-increasing accuracy and detail, aimed perhaps more at the adult collector since this is what those children had become. The manufacturers were clearly on to a good thing until Matchbox discovered that they could sell an almost infinite number of identical vans, provided that they regularly introduced new logos for them. Eventually the collectors revolted and depressed a market which has never fully recovered since.

A Spitfire and Hurricane for Rupert and Bill, Christmas 1943.

Annuals

During the war the kind of quality toys that were entirely absent from the shops survived in the realm of children's literature. I have a Tiny Tots Annual from the early days of the War and the illustration on its cover depicts a boy and girl sitting up in bed on Christmas morning with a toy train, car and aeroplane of a kind that one could only dream about at the time. Inside my 1943 Rupert Annual there is a story, illustrated by the incomparable Alfred Bestall, of how Rupert and Bill Badger travelled to Santa's workshop where they helped paint toy aircraft for other children to be given at Christmas. Rupert tells Bill to paint the Hurricanes while he paints the Spitfires and the two are eventually rewarded when they discover that Father Christmas has given one of the fighter aircraft to each of them, both of which were rather oddly painted black.

Then Rupert proudly shows his plane,
And tells the strange tale once again.

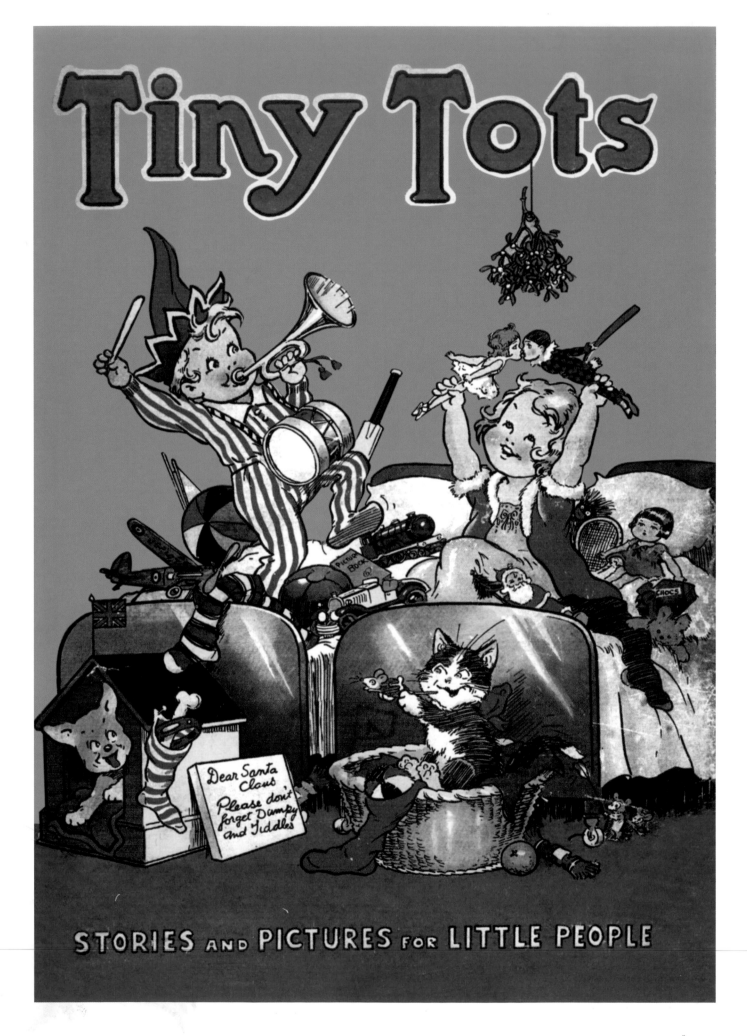

The only actual model planes that I came across either during or immediately after the war consisted of set of plans and pieces of soft balsa wood which one was supposed to carve and sandpaper to the appropriate shape! I always ended up with cuts and bruises and not much else!

Opposite: Wartime annual 'Tiny Tots'

A push-along train

Another favourite toy was a train made by Tri-ang which I could sit on and push along with my feet. It was mainly made of wood but had a metal boiler and it was painted red. It was a simple representation of a tank locomotive with four improbably small wheels with rubber tyres. I remember that it made a very satisfying rasping sound as it went along although it wasn't remotely like any that a real steam locomotive could ever make. Tri-ang was of course owned by Lines Bros and many years later I had the privilege of being shown around the Hornby and Scalextric factory in Margate by Richard Lines.

"Blackout" Cards.

"Blackout"

A wartime board game called "Blackout" has somehow survived not only the war itself but, even more remarkably, all the years that have followed since. The streets of London are depicted on a black board and there are playing cards which represent Air Raid Wardens, War Auxiliary Policemen and the Auxiliary Fire Squad. Others cards feature sandbags, fire buckets, fire fighting equipment and fire alarms. Finally there are traffic light cards with narrow crosses which represent the lights at red, amber and green and were intended to be too faint for any enemy aircraft flying overhead to see. Presumably sharp eyed motorists were able to make out these wartime traffic lights through the London smog but it must have made life extremely difficult for them. "Blackout" was a cheery way to pass the nights away in the air raid shelter while the British fighter aircraft took on the German bombers over our heads!

Sexton Blake

Less worrying perhaps, was a pack of cards, that has also survived, and which has to do with cops and robbers and the indomitable sleuth Sexton Blake with his assistant Tinker. Sexton Blake on the side of the goodies and the arch villain called "The Boss" are each rated at 120 points while various members of the police force and criminal fraternity are worth fewer points. As with "Blackout" I have forgotten the rules but I imagine that the game must have been simple to play.

Sexton Blake Card Game.

The Cinematograph

One toy that survived in our home from before the war was a cinematograph. These were the days before television and, having a powerful light bulb inside it, the machine was able to project moving pictures on the wall of a darkened room. It was worked by a handle at the side so that the film could be slowed down, speeded up, or made to pause. My brother David and I would snoop around the alleys at the side of the Eastleigh's Regal and Odeon cinemas and rescue the short lengths of film which had been cut out and thrown away when, as frequently happened, the film being shown had broken down. The result was that we had some intriguing sequences which were without a beginning or an end. In one a woman was watching from a darkened house while a car approached up the broad drive with its headlights sweeping both the lawn and the window where she stood with the curtains drawn back. Was he a friend or a foe and what would be her fate when he arrived? She seemed to be apprehensive as she looked through the window. In another short snip from a feature-length film, boys were having a snowball fight in a school playground and one snowball, containing a concealed stone, caused the victim's face to bleed. What punishment resulted from the dastardly deed remained unknown but it all looked very sinister and premeditated.

My first Hornby Train set

I was given an 0 gauge Hornby train set just after the War when the company only produced the least expensive items from its pre-war range. It came in a box with an

0-4-0 Hornby trains from the 1920s and 1930s with a Bassett-Lowke station.

ambitious illustration on its cover of a 4-6-0 express locomotive pulling a rake of eight-wheeled coaches but inside was a simple 0-4-0 train with a four-wheel tender, two four-wheeled wagons and a circle of rails with a very tight radius. It was a green No.20 and carried the number 2595 on the sides of its tender, which was in fact the number of the 4-6-2 LNER locomotive Trigo. The overall length of the loco and tender was a modest eight and a half inches. The clockwork motor was more than adequate for its purpose and the train shot around the track at such a rate that it threatened to leap from the rails. It always seemed to me to be like a caged animal and I would have loved to have been able to extend its track. Off the rails its wheels would spin impotently on lino and just wouldn't go at all on the carpet. But, winding up its spring and placing it on its rails, I had tremendous fun with it and used to pile farm animals into its wagons before sending them on their journey.

Motor races in Hampshire

I have already mentioned the Dinky Toys which my brother and I eagerly sought amongst the gifts from Father Christmas. In my book *When Motor Racing was Fun* I describe the races that were held in our garden by my brother David, our friend Keith and myself with some of the Dinky Toy models, after we had gone to Goodwood on Easter Monday in 1949 to watch some real races. For those who have not read my earlier book I will describe it briefly again here.

The only means of propulsion we possessed for these cars lay literally in our own hands. We oiled their axles liberally to make them run more smoothly and then, after pushing them firmly backwards and forwards several times between our thumbs and forefingers, we would release them at speed over the cemented area of the back garden and on to the lawn beyond. Eventually the holes in the centre of the wheels would become so enlarged that they fell off the ends of the axles and these then had to be replaced with sections of bicycle spokes which we crimped at the ends. Each of us had three Dinky Toy racing cars painted in team colours and each of their runs represented one lap of a Grand Prix. Their positions were carefully recorded and, after the requisite number of runs had been made by all the cars, the results were announced. Each of the events in the Grand Prix Season had its place in our calendar and a World Champion emerged at the end of the year. David's 23c Mercedes Benz was most successful overall but my 23f Alfa Romeos performed as well as any of the others, painted green and made to represent V16 BRMs. A Monte Carlo Rally was held each winter using road cars like the 36b Bentley and the 36d Rover, with extravagant use of sand, earth and water to create the right conditions. I am ashamed to admit that this caused the headlamps to break from the radiators of some of the 36 Series cars and it also inevitably took its toll on their paintwork.

Looking back now I wonder at how much fun we had with these simple toy cars. There was no television to distract us and we used our creative imagination and ingenuity to create the fun ourselves. It just couldn't happen today.

3
FROM LITTLE ACORNS

THE WORD TOY is derived from an old English word meaning tool and originally referred to the miniatures which belonged to adults rather than children, but Pieter Brueghel's famous painting 'Children's Games' shows them playing with toys as long ago as 1560, and I suspect that there never was a time when children didn't play with toys. Toys must certainly have pre-dated the invention of the wheel, but what makes me believe that toys are as old as the human race itself is the way kittens will make a toy of anything that moves. Unlike humans, animals are unable to progress from one generation to the next, building on the experience of their forebears, and so we may assume that their behaviour has always been very much as it is today. Cats must always have played with mice no matter how well they were fed, not just because they regarded them as their next meal, but because they simply enjoyed the fun of it, and they must always have continued to try to coax the lifeless bodies of mice into activity long after they were capable of any further movement. Young animals play in order to equip themselves to become hunters when they are fully grown and, without carrying the comparison between young animals and children too far, it is the case that when children play 'doctors and nurses', with or without their toy stethoscopes and thermometers, they also imitate the behaviour of their elders. More importantly, children, like young animals, must always have enjoyed play for play's sake. Who can say when children first picked up small flat stones to see how many times they could make them bounce off the surface of a sea or a lake?

Spinning tops

In her excellent book *The History of Toys* Deborah Jaffe refers to the theory of D.W. Gould that the origin of the spinning top can be traced to the sycamore seed pods that spin as they fall to the ground, and to the fire makers who spun a thin spindle of wood between their hands to create fire through friction.

Others have said that the spinning top was first invented when children discovered that they could make an acorn spin on the ground between their thumbs and forefingers. Of course no one was around at the time to photograph it and none could record it in print. But I am prepared to accept that this was the case and that eventually someone hit upon the idea of shaping a piece of wood so that it was wide at one end and pointed at the other to make it perform more satisfactorily than an acorn as a spinning top. No doubt it was many centuries later that the lathe, worked at first by hand, made it possible to produce the shape of a spinning top much more quickly and easily, and with far greater precision.

Plunger tops

It is possible to say with much more accuracy that the plunger top arrived during the course of the nineteenth century when the Industrial Revolution transformed the manufacture of toys as it did that of everything else. The use of metal was essential for plunger tops as they incorporated a mechanism which caused them to spin each time the plunger was depressed. No one knows who first thought of cutting holes in the side of these tops so that they would make a whistling noise as they spun. It was probably at about the same time that it was found that by painting the tops in two distinct colours a third would be created as they spun. Children, being children, must soon have started to compete with each other to see which one could sustain the spin of these tops the longest, while the lone player could also try to push the boundaries of his or her personal best.

Conkers

Acorns were readily available in prehistoric times and so too were horse chestnuts. I defy anyone to say who first had the presence of mind to pierce a horse chestnut right through the middle with a skewer and then to thread it with a piece of string tied at one end to make a conker. I will concede that someone must have invented the skewer or something very like one first, but playing with conkers has a long and honourable history even if, in more recent times, some have been known to cheat by soaking their conkers in vinegar!

Whipping tops

In the course of the development of spinning tops someone had the bright idea of using a length of string to give them renewed momentum by whipping them from the side as they spun, and so the whipping top was invented. It is not an easy skill for anyone to acquire but, with children, the harder the challenge the greater is the fun in mastering it. Of course whipping a top can be the quickest way to bring its progress to a sudden and inglorious end, but it is that possibility which makes it all worth the effort, and competing with others to see who can keep his or her top going the longest has always added to the fun and excitement. Further progress was made with the addition of a metal spring which made it possible to wind the top up before setting it on the ground to let it spin. No doubt the purists would have regarded this as cheating!

Yo Yos

Yo yos are depicted on the walls of the Egyptian temples and were popular in ancient Greece where they were made of wood, metal and terra cotta and decorated. Both the Duke of Wellington and the Emperor Napoleon enjoyed yo yos. They were first patented by James Haven and Charles Hettrich in 1866, and in the 1920s Pedro Flores, a Philippine immigrant, gave displays with them at a Santa Monica hotel where he was a bellboy. He founded a company and gave the toy its name which means "come come". Donald Duncan bought Flores's company in 1929 and introduced the first plastic models in the 1950s.

Skipping ropes

Skipping or jumping ropes also have a long history. They were used in ancient Egypt from 1600BC, and possibly much earlier than that in China. I never tried my hand with skipping ropes when I was a child, partly because it seemed to be rather a girlie thing to do, and partly because girls were so much better at doing it than boys, but I don't deny that both boys and girls enjoyed skipping in their school playgrounds, or that they can both become extremely proficient at it. Skipping can involve two ropes held in parallel with two children to hold them, one at each end, who revolve them around in opposite directions so that other children can jump over or under them.

It represents an excellent way to keep fit which is cheap, requires little space, and encourages interaction between the children. I suspect that skipping is one of those pastimes which is subject to crazes so that there will be times when every child will be at it and others when there will be none.

Noah's arks

Noah's arks were popular at least three hundred years ago and they belonged to an age when the Bible had a much greater influence on most people's lives than is the case today. When they first found their way into homes the Bible was often read aloud with all the family sitting around the dining room table to listen. Most of those who repeatedly heard familiar passages read to them would have felt that they knew some of the figures in the Old Testament better than they knew their own next door neighbours. Many people acquired a detailed knowledge of the story of

Noah's ark and, accepting the account of the Flood in the Book of Genesis without question, they regarded the description of the animals entering the ark two-by-two as being historically true.

Noah's ark, with all the different species of animals that were involved, made an excellent subject for toy makers and these toys, which were handled with appropriate reverence, were brought out to be enjoyed on Sundays. It was thought that they were spiritually uplifting for the children of the household as well as providing them with good innocent fun.

They were also considered to be educational toys because of all the different kinds of animals, and they had a particular appeal to children because of their construction in the form of a ship.

Most of the early Noah's arks were made in Germany and, although they were individually constructed in what began as a cottage industry, they conformed to a small number of basic designs. They bore no trade marks and so it is impossible to identify their makers today.

The earliest arks were made from wood or straw and were either flat bottomed, which meant that their superstructure stood on a thin base which extended at each end and was shaped to make the bow and stern of a ship, or they had properly shaped hulls which made them look more like boats. In each case at least one side of the pitched roof would open with a hinge so that the figures could be stored inside when it was not in use. Frequently a dove was placed at the top of the roof with a twig in its beak to conform to the account in the Book of Genesis.

The metal arks of the nineteenth century were hand painted or lithographed and, in the case of more expensive examples, the animals were rounded in shape to look much more realistic than those cut out of flat pieces of wood. At this later stage arks were often professionally manufactured by the toy makers and they were marketed alongside model trains and motor cars by the big London stores.

A doll's house, dolls and a Noah's ark in Bygones, St Marychurch, Torquay.

4
TOYS FOR TODDLERS

Dolls

No ONE CAN SAY WHEN DOLLS were first invented but they can be traced back to the very earliest times. The word doll comes from a Greek word meaning idol and it is probable that the first dolls were used for religious purposes rather than for play, but one authority, Constance Eileen King, believes that children played with dolls from the beginning. Whatever may be the truth of that, dolls have been found in Egyptian graves which are more than 2000 years old. They have also been discovered in the graves of the ancient Romans and Greeks and, while this association may appear to be macabre, it most probably signifies that Roman and Greek children enjoyed playing with their dolls when they were alive and well, and the fact that dolls were placed

Dolls and teddy bears in a scene from Harrods.
Courtesy Company Archive Harrods Limited

in the graves of children shows just how important they must have been to them. The earliest dolls were made of wood or clay and there is evidence that as long ago as 600BC some had moveable arms and legs, and also clothes. Wooden dolls have been found in Europe dating from the sixteenth century and during the course of the succeeding century they were produced with realistically carved faces, jointed limbs, and attractive clothes.

By the thirteenth century town fairs, such as the Leipzig Fair in Germany and the Smithfield Fair in England, were important in providing markets for dolls and other toys such as rattles and spinning tops and hobby horses. Nicholas Orme has described how children treated as dolls the figures of saints which were thrown out of many churches and monasteries during the Reformation. In contrast to the crudely-made wooden peg dolls which were fashioned from one piece of wood and were without legs, examples of more refined dolls were made with paper soaked in water and firmly compressed. It was from this process that papier mache dolls were developed and they proved to be remarkably strong and durable. Glue and sawdust were added to the compressed mixture to make it even more robust.

After this came the practice of pouring moulten wax into moulds to make very realistic dolls' heads. These were made in London by Montanari and Pierotti who also added glass eyes and hair which in some cases came from human heads and was therefore extremely realistic. The wax heads and limbs were then sewn to stuffed cloth bodies.

Porcelain heads and bodies began to appear in the nineteen century made of glazed china or bisque, some being sold in an unpainted state while others were painted before being fired for a second time. France led the field in making fine and realistic dolls but, in addition, a thriving German doll industry centred around Thuringia. Simon and Halbig were founded in 1869 and Armand Marseille some twenty years later.

The French firm of Jumeau made dolls with bisque heads and composition bodies, and in 1899 several enterprising French manufacturers of dolls combined to form an association so as to be better able to compete with the more successful German companies. Fashionable dolls were more often bought by or for ladies for their own pleasure rather than that of their children and, in consequence, enormous care was taken with the manufacture of their fashionable clothes.

Rag dolls were popular with small children and many of these were made by their own mothers and aunts.

The Hyatt Brothers in the United States of America were the first to adopt celluloid in the manufacture of dolls in mid 1860s. They poured the celluloid to line two moulds which represented the two halves of a head and then joined them together by the application of heat where they met. The main problem with this was that the celluloid was highly inflammable and it also tended to fade when it was exposed to the light. As a result of this plastic was introduced early in the twentieth century and, by the 1950s this was in turn replaced by vinyl.

Baby dolls have been the favourite toys and closest companions of young girls for years but it could be said that dolls came of age when Barbie burst upon the scene from California in 1959. She was enormously popular with children but predictably became the object of fierce and bitter criticism from many adults because she taught young girls to try to look ultra slim and very grown up. Of course the adverse comments had no greater effect upon Barbie than it did upon the models on the catwalks, and it was not long before the British firm Pedigree of Lines Brothers launched Sindy to compete with her.

It is one of the ironies of history that in 1966, just as the West was moving towards an era in which girls and boys were supposed to share the same interests, Action Man was invented. In truth the boys who played with Action Man with his multiplicity of uniforms and weapons would have been deeply offended if they had ever been accused of playing with dolls. It was all serious stuff for them, while at the same time being great fun, and plastic jeeps and other military vehicles were thoughtfully provided by the manufacturers to add to their enjoyment. I can remember scouring the shops of Southampton and Portsmouth one December weekend before tracking down what appeared to be the last Action Man tank left in all the shops in the South of England! Sindy, of course, was not to be outdone, and could be seen around the same time driving her E Type Jaguar!

Doll's Houses

Albert V, the Duke of Barvaria is said to have been responsible for the manufacture of the very first doll's house in the later half of the sixteenth century. It was intended for his own amusement and

DOLLS MANSIONS.

Handsome Dolls House.   As illustration.

With 4 rooms, windows fitted with curtains, balcony on first floor
Beautifully enamelled and finished, imitation tile roof and brick walls.

30 in. High.   25 in. Wide.   20 in. Deep.

Price **42/-**

Handsome Villa.   As illustration.

With 4 rooms and staircase, imitation electric door bell to ring, all windows
fitted with curtains, doors to open, imitation tile roof and brick walls

Beautifully finished.   31½ in. High,   30½ in. Wide,   20 in. Deep

Price   ..   **59 6**

Doll House.   As illustration.

Beautifully enamelled and finished

With 5 rooms and staircase, all doors to open, fitted with imitation electric door
bell to ring. All windows fitted with curtains, imitation tile roof

38 in. High   35   Wide,   26 in. Deep.

Price   ..   **97,6**

Superior Model Dolls House.

With 5 rooms, windows fitted with curtains, 1 window at rear of house
imitation tile roof and brick walls.

Strongly made and well finished.

36 in. High,   29 in. Wide,   19 in. Deep.

Price   ..   **49 6**

Carriage extra on all Dolls' Houses outside London Carrier Radius.

Doll's Houses in the Gamages
Catalogue in 1912.

that of his guests rather than for children, and it was a miniature copy of the great house in which
he lived. In the two hundred years that followed doll's houses with detailed interiors became
popular throughout England and Germany but, as yet, they remained models to be displayed by
their owners for their friends to admire and for children not to touch. The object of those who
bought them was still to display miniature houses which were, as far as was possible, small scale
replicas of their residences. In addition individual rooms were made for the very different purpose
of instructing young girls how they should do the work of a house keeper, and models of shops
were made for the similar purpose of instructing new shop assistants. Deborah Jaffe records that
in 1572 the Princesses of Saxony were given a miniature pewter kitchen with a full compliment
of cooking vessels.

In Victorian times doll's houses were at last made for the amusement of young children, and
Queen Victoria made them fashionable in England with her beautiful doll's house which can be
seen in Osborne House on the Isle of Wight. Some fine doll's houses were featured in the stores'
catalogues in the early twentieth century and Lines Brothers produced a range of miniature
houses at affordable prices. Miniature shops were made so that children could learn how to handle
money.

In more recent years many fathers, including the author, built doll's houses for their young daughters from scratch and were able to purchase accessories such as metal windows, doors and chimneys to give them a more professional finish. More recently, specialist firms have produced doll's houses in kit form so that those who lack any special skills in carpentry are able to produce very satisfactory results with glue, paint, and a very careful examination of the instructions. The most difficult part is attempting to paint the interior walls after the doll's house has been assembled. Doll's house furniture abounds today and the quality is so good that a great many of these miniature homes are constructed and furnished by adults for their own amusement, which takes the story of the doll's house full circle.

Doll's tea sets

The first mention of a doll's tea set is found in the sixteenth century when these miniature tea sets were made in Germany of copper or pewter. Similar sets were made elsewhere in Europe of gold and silver and, from the eighteenth century onwards, of fine china and porcelain.

As was the case with so many toys, it was the Industrial Revolution of the mid nineteenth century that enabled doll's tea sets to become accessible to a much larger number of children and by the end of that century they were also made in celluloid and bakelite. It must surely have been in England, when everything stopped for tea, that doll's tea sets were most popular, and with the advent of plastic they were produced even more cheaply. Plastic cups and saucers, moreover, offered the advantage of being almost unbreakable so they outlasted those which had been much more delicately crafted in china. It is not hard to imagine how tea parties would frequently take place, with the dolls and teddy bears made to sit in a circle while their young owners helped themselves to all the tea and the cakes.

Doll's prams

It was inevitable that the toy makers of Germany would one day provide the growing number of dolls in Europe and beyond with their own prams, and by the end of the nineteenth century they manufactured prams which were miniature replicas of the full-sized ones. They were imported by the London stores, while Silver Cross, famous for the full-sized perambulators it made for babies, was not slow to produce miniature models for dolls as well. Before the Second World War Silver Cross pram bodies were made of wood with a metal chassis and wheels, but having had to make aluminium panels for Spitfires during the War the company produced dolls prams of that material when peace was restored.

Teddy bears

One would have thought that Robert Southey's story of Goldilocks and the Three Bears, which he wrote in 1837, would have done nothing to endear those potentially aggressive animals to small children and that, instead, it would have had the effect of reinforcing a healthy respect for their less cuddly attributes. However sixty years later the German company Gebruder Sussenguth made a stuffed toy in the form of a bear and in 1896 the first bears of Margarete Steiff appeared.

In fact Margarete Steiff, who had been afflicted with polio at the age of two and was confined to a wheel chair, made her first stuffed toy in the form of an elephant in 1879, and she developed a whole range of toys modelled on different animals in the years that followed. By the time that her first bear appeared she was employing a staff of nearly forty.

Soon afterwards, her nephew, Richard Steiff, sent her some sketches for an upright bear which she seized upon and modelled. Then Theodore Roosevelt, the President of the United States, inadvertently became responsible for creating a huge affection for Teddy Bears. It began with an incident in 1902, when Roosevelt mercifully declined to shoot a young bear cub while hunting its parents. This 'kindly' gesture by the President became common knowledge soon afterwards when Clifford K Berryman drew a cartoon of the incident for the *Washington Post* in November that year. This in turn prompted Morris and Rose Michtom to ask the United States President the following year if they could name a stuffed bear after him which they intended to produce in large numbers. "Teddy" Roosevelt told them that he doubted whether the name would be of any use at all in promoting their product, but it proved to be a marketing triumph! In fact Roosevelt was so impressed with the public's reaction to the first Teddy Bear that he had the "The Teddy Bears Picnic" played throughout his next election campaign!

Teddy bears were becoming big business and Herman Borgford, the representative of the New York department store of George Borgfeldt, ordered three thousand of Margarete's Steiff's jointed teddy bears. None of these is thought to have survived but they assured the future of Steiff bears. Other firms sought to capitalise on their appeal so that the manufacture of bears had come a long way from the time when they were the product of a tiny cottage industry. The famous trade mark metal button in the ear of Steiff products was blank to begin with but became embossed with an elephant as early as 1905 in deference to the fact that Margarete's first stuffed toy had been made in that form. Steiff's trademark is still "Knopf in Ohr" or "Button in the Ear". Over one million teddy bears had been made by Steiff by the end of 1907 and of course they have gained greatly in value because of the interest of collectors.

Winnie the Pooh

Alan Alexander Milne's *Winnie the Pooh* appeared for the first time in the *London Evening News* in 1925 and, almost as important as the author, was E. H. Shepard, a cartoonist for *Punch* magazine, who was responsible for drawing the illustrations of Pooh and his friends. Shepard based his drawings on the rather battered toys in Milne's son Christopher's toy cupboard, and the name Winnie derived from a live bear called Winnipeg which was the mascot of the 2nd Canadian Infantry Brigade in the First World War. Pooh was a name which Alan Milne and Christopher had given to a swan.

The driver says, "My car I'll show;
This giant mainspring makes it go."

A 1943 clockwork car.

Some stuffed toys which are true to the drawings of E. H. Shepard have been made but, after Walt Disney bought the rights to them in 1961, Pooh, Eeyore, Piglet and the others re-emerged both on film and in the toy shops bearing little resemblance to the characters that were created in 1925. E. H. Shepard placed it on record that Disney's Pooh bear was "a complete travesty". I believe that it would have been better if the great Disney empire had given its entertaining little characters entirely different names because then it wouldn't have given offence to the genuine lovers of the original Winnie the Pooh.

Rupert Bear

Rupert Bear was created by Mary Toutel and first appeared on 8 November 1920 in the *Daily Express* newspaper to compete with the *Daily Mirror's* strip cartoon about Pip, Squeak and Wilfred. In 1935 the artist Alfred Bestall was asked to stand in for Mary as her eyes were beginning to fail, and he continued to draw the adventures of Rupert Bear and his friends for the next thirty years. For me, as for many of my contemporaries, no one who followed Alfred Bestall could possibly compare with him. I looked for my *Rupert Bear Annual* every year throughout the war and afterwards, enjoying Bestall's beautiful art work and imaginative tales. Amongst the most memorable images that Bestall created in the war years was of a car which had a clockwork motor and an enormous spring mounted horizontally immediately behind the driver. No real harm came to the inventive motorist when the spring broke and sent him soaring into the sky on the end of it. No one ever came to any real harm in Rupert Bear, least of all the plucky bear with a stout heart. But for a very young boy the adventures were capable of conveying an air of menace strong enough to make them exciting.

Walt Disney has not yet turned his particular attention to Bestall's bear and Rupert is still to be seen, in his annuals and at the toy shops, with his familiar red jumper and yellow scarf and trousers.

Noddy

Enid Blyton's Noddy.

Enid Blyton wrote six hundred books for children and sixty million copies were sold worldwide. Her books were translated into seventy different languages. Yet, in spite of her phenomenal success, she was heavily criticised by the literary elite who said that her writing was immature and racist, and this led to her books being banned from some public libraries. For all that she taught many like me, who grew up with the exciting stories of the Famous Five, to love English literature at a very early age. Enid Blyton introduced Noddy in 1949 with *Little Noddy goes to Toyland* when her illustrator was Van Der Beek, and Noddy remains enormously popular both as a toy and as the subject of an endless flow of children's stories.

Paddington Bear

Paddington Bear was created by Michael Bond and his artist was Peggy Fortnum when, on 13 October 1958, the first of fourteen books was published with the title *A Bear called Paddington*. Bond was inspired by Winnie the Pooh to create a gentle and polite little bear who, always with the best of intentions, repeatedly found himself to be in trouble. Habitually misunderstood, Paddington came from darkest Peru with his battered suitcase filled with marmalade sandwiches, and he wore a felt hat, duffle coat and Wellington boots. His adventures made the transition from books to television where his popularity continued to grow and he was soon to be found in toy shops as a rather more firm than cuddly toy in various sizes. Long may he continue to maintain the character that Bond and Fortnum have given to him.

Michael Bond's
Paddington Bear.

Rocking Horses

Hobby horses are known to have existed both in Persia and ancient Greece from about 400BC, but the earliest known rocking horse belonged to King Charles I in the seventeenth century. Some believe that the rocking horse was a natural progression from the wooden cradles which were rocked to and fro to get babies to sleep and, in the course of time, the horses came to be realistically carved and painted. By the end of the eighteenth century the wood of many rocking horses was covered in a material which gave them a smooth finish and made them resemble the real horses that occupied the stables outside. Initially all rocking horses were mounted on curved wooden runners so that children could rock them back and forth, imagining perhaps that they were leaping over hedges and fences chasing a fox. Then in 1880 Philip Marqua patented the safety stand which stood firmly and immovably on the floor while the horse could be ridden backwards and forwards on top of it. Rocking horses of both types were marketed by Gamages, Harrods and Hamleys from the early years of the twentieth century, and Lines Brothers was not slow to develop examples at popular prices. It is difficult to see how rocking horses will ever entirely lose their appeal but realistically crafted pedal cars gained in popularity at their expense in the increasingly mechanised world of the twentieth century.

Edwardian Rocking Horse in
Bygones, St Marychurch,
Torquay.

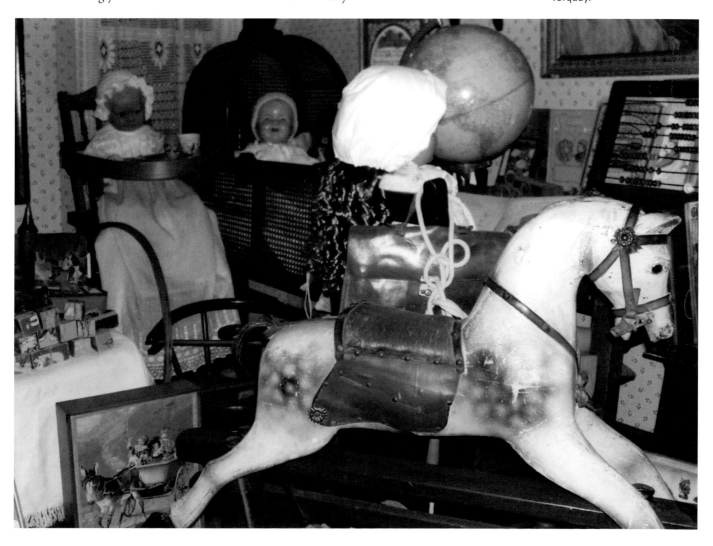

Pedal Cars

The first pedal cars were made at the very beginning of the twentieth century if not a little earlier and they were constructed by craftsmen in small numbers in Germany. Like the early model below which I was fortunate to acquire in perfect condition in the 1970s, they had wooden bodies which were often professionally finished to the standard of coach built motor cars. The chassis was made of metal as were the spoked wheels, while the rims of their steering wheels were often of wood and of small diameter. The pedal cars ran on narrow rubber tyres and they were equipped with beautifully-crafted upholstered seats. My veteran pedal car lacked any trade mark but, judging by the quality of its construction and not least its finely lined paintwork, it must have been the product of one of the foremost manufacturers.

Veteran pedal car.

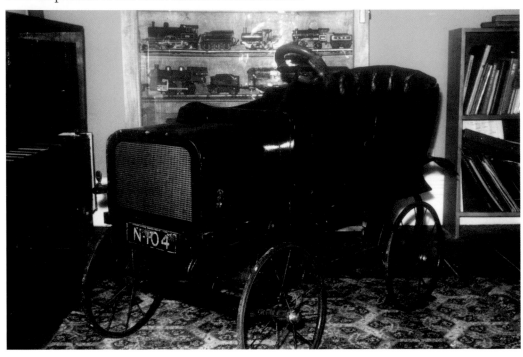

The early catalogues of the London stores contain a range of fine pedal cars mostly, it must be assumed, of German manufacture.

Elsewhere in Europe, Giodani made pedal cars immediately after the First World War in Italy. Eureka was equally well known in France for its pedal cars and its earliest models were made in 1922. Eureka's output in 1953 amounted to 53 000 which suggests that the rocking horses had by this time been all but eclipsed.

From 1906 the Reo Motor Company in the United States made pedal cars which were replicas of the full scale cars manufactured by them for the motoring public and their primary object was to promote the sales of these cars.

Margarete Steiff, although best known for her teddy bears, also made pedal cars between 1927 and 1942 and her range of high quality models, which boasted metal bodies, included the Tretmobil, the Tripmobil, the Sportmobil and the Tempomobil.

The veteran pedal car with Richard, Wendy and Candy.

In England Tri-ang of Lines Bros Ltd was prolific in its production of pedal cars, many of which represented the products of the British motor industry. *The Collector's All-colour Guide to Toy Cars* by Gordon Gardiner and Richard O'Neill contains photographs of their red "Comet" made in the 1930s, a simple model with chrome radiator, solid wheels and a horn, and a very much more impressive "Brooklands No 8" with a rounded radiator, spoked wheels, Dunlop Cord pneumatic tyres, louvred bonnet sides and pointed tail. Also shown in that book is a 1931 "Buick Regal" by Tri-ang which had an authentic radiator, four battery-powered headlamps at the front and side which were operated by a switch on the dashboard, an opening door with a cast metal door handle, a perspex windscreen with a

Left and below: Pedal cars in the National Motor Mesum, Beaulieu.

chromed frame, a rear view mirror, a front bumper and number plate and sprung suspension. Tri-ang didn't overlook Rolls Royce and did justice to the "best car in the world" with an electrically powered model in the early 1930s which was capable of running for up to fifteen miles without having its battery re-charged. It had working lights at the front, back and sides, a chrome radiator, a louvred bonnet, hand brake and forward and reverse gears.

In the '30s Tri-ang also produced pedal cars which were unmistakably modelled on a Bullnose Morris, a Lagonda, a Vauxhall, and a Citroen. Particularly impressive was their Fraser Nash with tubular chassis. and distinctive Fraser Nash-style body. After the war the firm offered a pedal car which was a poor representation of the Vanwall racing car and a Ford Zephyr which, though bearing no resemblance to the cars that were made in Dagenham, were loved by children. They also made fire engines, tractors and jeeps. Pedal cars remained popular and Tri-ang produced them in large numbers, equipping them with horns and sirens which represented excellent play value and probably meant more to their young drivers than the authenticity of their design.

In the 1980s Sharna Tri-ang made a splendid and very expensive Rolls Royce Corniche with an electric motor and two forward gears.

Richard in a Tri-ang pedal car in 1967.

Two notable pedal cars were manufactured after the war by the Austin Motor Company and they were based on actual Austin models. One was called the J40 Roadster and was clearly modelled on the A40 Austin Devon saloon and the other, called the Pathfinder Special, was a model of an open-wheeled Austin Seven racing car called the Jamieson OHV 750 which had raced at Brooklands before the war. These cars were constructed by disabled coal miners in a factory in Bargoed in South Wales built solely for this purpose in 1949. The Pathfinder was the first model to be produced at Bargoed and its place was taken the next year by the J40. They were beautifully engineered to Longbridge standards, long before the arrival of British Leyland, and could sometimes be seen displayed in the Austin car showrooms. Both models were 5 ft 3 in long. The model engine details included sparking plugs and leads. They cost £33, which was far from cheap at the time, but over 32 000 of the J40s were made before production ceased in 1971.

Above left: Austin Pathfinder
Special and *(right)* Austin J40
Roadster in the National
Motor Museum, Beaulieu.

In the years since the Second World War Audi offered a replica of the 1930s C Type Auto Union for children priced at 9700 Euros.

Toy soldiers

William Britain came originally from the Midlands but moved to north-east London in 1846 where he made and marketed mechanical toys in competition with the great German toy makers. In the 1890s he decided to specialise in making toy soldiers, and his son William developed the process of producing them from hollow castings. Father and son presented them to the market place in 1883, and William senior was also assisted in his business by the other members of his large family which, in addition to William Junior, consisted of Alfred, Frederick, Frank, Edward, Emily and Anne. After a slow start William Britain and his family became firmly established and the demand for his products exceeded the numbers they could supply.

Gamages provided an important outlet for Britain, and a mark of his spectacular success was the fact that in only few years William Britain manufactured nearly all the toy soldiers that Gamages stocked. In 1906, Gamages could boast that it stocked no less than 500 000, mostly Britains', toy soldiers. The store asked its customers to note that all its Britain's soldiers were in fact made in England, that they were made to the same scale, and that all the uniforms were correct in every detail. To be truthful, Britains actually produced toy soldiers in two sizes to be compatible with both gauge I and gauge 0.

At the turn of the century Britains moved up a gear in expanding its range of products. For this to happen its premises in Lambton Road was demolished and replaced with a purpose-built factory which employed a staff of three hundred.

The production of toy soldiers stopped for the First World War when, sadly, munitions were required for full scale soldiers and, after the war, the public was understandably less enthusiastic about military toys than it had previously been. In response to this Britains directed its energies towards the production of model farmers and their animals with its new Home Farm Range.

This proved highly popular so that a new factory, known as the North Light Building, was built in Walthamstow for making the farm models and many of its products were sold in the United States. In the 1930s, when economic times were hard, Britains adapted to these circumstances by widening its range to model gardens, complete with borders and flowers, circus animals and circus vehicles, until war once again intervened. After the war plastics dominated the market and eventually took the place of metal in Britains products.

The Herald Company was taken over by Britains in 1959 and this led to the parent company having a greater capacity to producing plastic farm figures and its extremely popular range of diecast farm vehicles.

In more recent years Britains manufactured fine quality diecast soldiers for collectors and in 1997 it was taken over by Ertl who ensured the future development of this important range.

Opposite: Britains Toy
Soldiers in Harrods Toy
Department, 1912.
Courtesy Company Archive
Harrods Limited

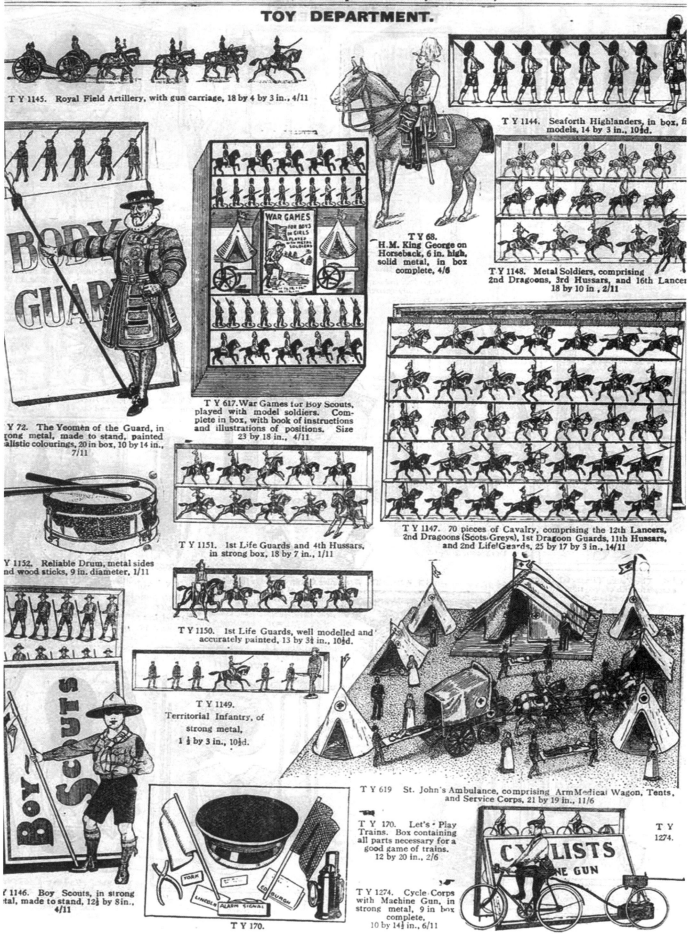

TOY DEPARTMENT.

T Y 1145. Royal Field Artillery, with gun carriage, 18 by 4 by 3 in., 4/11

T Y 1144. Seaforth Highlanders, in box, fi models, 14 by 3 in., 10½d.

Y 72. The Yeomen of the Guard, in strong metal, made to stand, painted realistic colourings, 20 in box, 10 by 14 in., 7/11

T Y 617. War Games for Boy Scouts, played with model soldiers. Complete in box, with book of instructions and illustrations of positions. Size 23 by 18 in., 4/11

WAR GAMES FOR BOYS OR GIRLS PLAYED WITH METAL SOLDIERS

T Y 68. H.M. King George on Horseback, 6 in. high, solid metal, in box complete, 4/6

T Y 1148. Metal Soldiers, comprising 2nd Dragoons, 3rd Hussars, and 16th Lancer 18 by 10 in , 2/11

Y 1152. Reliable Drum, metal sides and wood sticks, 9 in. diameter, 1/11

T Y 1151. 1st Life Guards and 4th Hussars, in strong box, 18 by 7 in., 1/11

T Y 1147. 70 pieces of Cavalry, comprising the 12th Lancers, 2nd Dragoons (Scots Greys), 1st Dragoon Guards, 11th Hussars, and 2nd Life Guards, 25 by 17 by 3 in., 14/11

T Y 1150. 1st Life Guards, well modelled and accurately painted, 13 by 3¼ in., 10½d.

T Y 1149. Territorial Infantry, of strong metal, 1½ by 3 in., 10½d.

T Y 619 St. John's Ambulance, comprising Arm Medical Wagon, Tents, and Service Corps, 21 by 19 in., 11/6

Y 1146. Boy Scouts, in strong tal, made to stand, 12½ by 8 in., 4/11

T Y 170.

T Y 170. Let's Play Trains. Box containing all parts necessary for a good game of trains. 12 by 20 in., 2/6

T Y 1274. Cycle Corps with Machine Gun, in strong metal, 9 in box complete, 10 by 14½ in., 6/11

T Y 1274.

THE TOYS MAKERS OF NUREMBERG

THE BARVARIAN TOWN OF NUREMBERG was situated where important trading routes crossed and reached out towards the four points of the compass. This, together with the fact that it was rich in pine forests which provided ideal timber for cutting and modelling, enabled Nuremberg to become the centre of Germany's toy industry. Local guilds were formed from the beginning of the fifteenth century to represent the region's craftsmen, and the Leipzig Imperial Fairs offered its toy makers the opportunity to showcase their wares before the world. With the coming of the Industrial Revolution such masters of the toy making industry as Marklin, Bing and Carette were enabled to work with metal to produce fine models of cars, boats and trains powered by clockwork, electric and steam.

A live-steam Bing locomotive with clockwork cars by Marklin and Carette.

5
THE BING BROTHERS

THE BROTHERS, IGNAZ AND ADOLF BING began their career in 1863 by selling the products of other companies, but they eventually became the largest of all the early German toy manufacturers in Nuremberg. Determined from the beginning to make their own models without the assistance of others, they became entirely independent of their suppliers at the earliest opportunity. They were driven by the conviction that they could produce toys and models that would be superior to those of their rivals, and their target was to show toys which they had manufactured themselves at the Bavarian Provincial Trade, Industry and Art Exhibition in 1882. In preparation for this they established their own works at 34 Kohnstrasse. Focused upon their goal they assembled a workforce of over a hundred full time workers within their factory and a similar number who worked part time in their own homes in the tradition of cottage industries. When the exhibition came to be staged the stand of the Bing brothers was seen to be larger than any of their rivals.

This was just the beginning, and Ignaz and Adolf acquired further premises in Untere Baustrasse and Hinterm Bahnof in Nuremberg along with a factory in Saxony which had previously made household goods. The Bings became a limited company called Gebr Bing A.G and its earliest trademark would be eagerly sought by collectors in later years.

Of crucial importance to the progress of Gebr Bing, was the visit of Wenman J Bassett-Lowke to the Paris Exhibition of 1900 where the Englishman was able to see their latest products. He was so impressed by their quality that Bassett-Lowke commissioned Bing to build models for him to sell in his shop at 112 High Holborn in London. The emphasis was on steam locomotives with the London and North Western Railway "Black Prince and "King Edward" being particularly prominent but, in addition to a growing range of British outline locomotives from 0 gauge to gauge IV, Bing tinplate cars, battleships, liners, submarines and stationary model steam engines also filled the shelves of the London shop, and the close cooperation between Bing and Bassett-Lowke, which is illustrated later on in this book, brought the products of Nuremberg to the attention of many discerning British fathers and their sons.

The number of Bing's employees grew steadily and amounted to some 5000 before the outbreak of the First World War.

In 1914 the Bing factories were taken over by the German Government for the war effort. The elder Bing brother, Ignaz died at the age of 79 before the war was over.

After the war the firm became Bing-Werke A,G and was run by Stephen Bing, Adolf's son. It continued to produce toys and models into the 1920s although, its near-scale model trains apart, something of the flare and inspiration of the founders seemed to be lacking in many of these later models, and discerning toy collectors today value more highly the toys that were made before the First World War. The Bassett-Lowke trademark came to be applied to the Bing products made for their London shop so that most of its customers were not aware that they had been made abroad.

Bing Trade Marks

1900-1902

1902-1914

1902-1914

After 1918

31

In 1928 offices were opened by Bing in Regensburger Strasse but then financial problems relating to the Wall Street crash and the Great Depression sent the firm into receivership. Bing managed to re-establish itself afterwards but its model railway department was taken over by Karl Bub with whom there had already been a working relationship, and Fleischmann acquired the production of its model ships.

Most Bing models, other than some of those which were produced specifically for Bassett-Lowke, carried the company's trademarks and they can be dated quite accurately according to their particular style. The ones most highly prized by collectors are those produced before 1902, but any Bing models made before 1914 are also extremely rare and desirable.

Bing cars, boats and trains ranged from inexpensive items made of thin lithographed tinplate to the more substantial models which were hand enamelled.

Today early Bing dreadnoughts, which measured up to a metre in length, are particularly rare. Powered by steam, they sat quite low in the water and some of them may have been launched from the sides of lakes more in hope than in expectation. Many sank without trace.

The Bing submarine rescued from the sea.
Courtesy *Southern Daily Echo*

The Bing submarine that was rescued from the English Channel

Back in 1975 a young man came to my door with a parcel underneath his arm. He had brought with him a model clockwork submarine which he had rescued from the English Channel. Being a diver, he had recently bought the wreck of a steam yacht which had sunk in the Channel a few miles out from Brighton in 1921 and, in one of his exploratory dives, he had discovered a large air pocket in one of the ship's cabins. Within the air pocket, and still perfectly dry fifty-four years after the ship had sunk, was the toy submarine. As soon as he had unpacked the boat in my study I saw that it had been made by Bing before the First World War and possibly as early as 1902. The familiar trade mark of that period was unmistakable and, with a little cleaning, it was seen to be in perfect condition. No doubt the fact that it was a hand painted model contributed to this, but the clockwork motor was also in perfect condition, not even requiring to be oiled! Painted grey with black trim and flying German flags, it was a remarkable find and Roger Quilter of the Solent News Agency ensured that it received the due attention of the *Southampton Daily Echo*. For a while the boat had a special place of honour in my collection, but it troubled me that the remains of its young owner had also been found in that pocket of air and, being unable in those circumstances to take any pleasure in the model, I passed the submarine on to another collector.

1905 cream De Dion

My very first Bing model was a medium sized De Dion car made in 1905 and I acquired it at an auction in Canterbury. The auctioneer had sent me a catalogue of the sale and, seeing that it included a number of pre-1914 cars, boats and trains, I set off from Southampton with my eldest brother John. Not having had any previous experience of auctions and being concerned that I might scratch my nose and find that I had unintentionally made a purchase, I had asked John to bid on my behalf for the items that interested me. When we arrived at the address in Canterbury the auction was already underway and we had to squeeze through the crowds that packed the rooms in order to catch a glimpse at the lots I had come to buy. I jotted down the amounts that represented my limit against each of those items in the catalogue but, being new to early tinplate toys, I had no idea how much they were really worth. I was encouraged at first by the fact that many of the lots, including sets of old *Encyclopaedia Britannicas*, were going for no more than a few pounds. However, when the first items that I had my eye on, which were three not enormously exciting Bing boats, came up for sale they all sailed far beyond the figures I had suggested for them. The same thing happened with all the railway items, which again were not of great rarity, and after this I indicated to John that he should keep on bidding for the three tinplate cars regardless of the cost, as I was determined not to go away empty handed. Of course this was quite the wrong thing to do at an auction, and the gasps of surprise and wonder which were heard around the packed auction room did nothing to settle my nerves. The bidding just went on and on with each of the three clockwork cars in turn as John carried on bidding until his was the only hand raised. The people in the crowd looked at us in astonishment as we gathering up my purchases and left the saleroom long before the sale had ended. I drove back to Southampton, with some concern that I might have paid far too much for the cars. However, within half an hour of returning home the phone rang and an eminent London collector, who later became a close friend, enquired about the cars I had bought. He had sent a representative to the sale and it was he who had been bidding against me. After I had described each of the three cars in detail he was able to assure me that they had all been bargains at the prices I paid. He mentioned that he had bought a fourth car, which I had overlooked because it was in several pieces and hidden in a biscuit tin. It was of course the rarest item in the whole sale, being a large Bing model of a Gordon Bennett racing car and he told me that he was hugely disappointed that the car was lacking the two tinplate figures of its driver and racing mechanic. I was able to tell him that the missing figures were jammed into the front seats of one of the cars of had bought! I promised to put them in the post to him the next day and so the two figures, one crouching over the car's steering wheel and the other holding on for his life, were reunited with their car.

 The cars I had purchased were a cream hand-enamelled 1905 Bing De Dion with part of one of its seats missing, a red 1908 Gunthermann saloon which lacked its bevelled glass windows and its original tinplate driver, and a blue 1908 Gunthermann limousine which was complete in every respect. Both the Gunthermann models were lithographed. I had the windows made for the red

1905 Bing De Dion

car by a local glazier, who was intrigued by my request, and I built up the missing part of the De Dion's seat which, after I had painted over the area where I had been working, looked quite presentable.

1902 blue Tonneau I

1902 Bing De Dion with rear door.

After the episode at Canterbury I made myself much better informed about the value of these early toys and then started to place advertisements for them in the newspapers. As a result of this a lady phoned me from an address in Sussex to tell me that, having recently bought an old house, she had found a toy car in its loft. From her description I realised that it had been made by Bing before 1905 and so I assured her that I would drive over to see it immediately. She said that the little footstep at the rear of the car had, only moments before, come away in her small son's hand and so I asked her to be sure to put the car right out of his reach! The car turned out to be a very rare toy indeed, in fact the only one of its kind to have come to the notice of the fraternity of collectors anywhere in the world! It was a 20cm long and hand enamelled 1902 Bing Tonneau with a door in the rear and a lamp mounted on the bonnet. I bought it and, as soon as I had returned home, glued the footstep back in place so that it was as good as new.

1903 cream Tonneau III

It was from another collector that I bought the largest example of a clockwork 1903 Bing Tonneau in cream. The car was massive in comparison to the blue one. It had two lamps, was lined in red, and had a green chassis. Best of all, it also had also survived the ravages of time in excellent condition. It has often been said that these early and expensive toys, which only found their way into the wealthiest of households, were brought out on Sundays, as had been the case with Noah's Arks years before, to be handled with supervision and care. This would explain why so many of them had remained in remarkably good condition.

1905 Bing De Dion.

1903 Bing Tonneau III.

1904 De Dion

My next purchase was another Bing De Dion. This was pale blue, much larger than the cream model I had bought in Canterbury, more attractive on account of both its size and colour, and in perfect condition. It was while I was staying in Charlestown in Cornwall, combining a family holiday with conducting the Sunday services, that I spotted the car in an antique shop. I readily agreed to pay the price that was asked and, thrilled with my purchase, placed it where it could be viewed in the vicarage until we returned to Southampton.

1902 horse-drawn fire-engine

One of the items illustrated in the 1902 Bassett-Lowke catalogue was a working model of a live-steam horse-drawn fire engine with a large vertical brass boiler. I had often looked at it and hoped that I might have the opportunity one day to acquire one. So I was more than pleased when one was offered to me in excellent condition, together with a large number of extremely early 0 gauge Marklin model railway items. The fire engine was 12 inches long without its shafts, 5 inches wide and 8 inches high and, in his catalogue, Mr W. J. Bassett-Lowke claimed that it was a vast improvement upon the usual run of those on the market. I entirely agreed with

him! Of course I never fired it up because, at the very least it would have caused damage to its paintwork and at worst it might have exploded!

1902 Bing Fire Engine.

1904 4-seater Mercedes Benz tourer

This was the star of my collection and remained, in my estimation, the finest toy that I ever possessed. It was a seriously large clockwork model of a Mercedes Benz touring car, no less than 42 cm long. I had received a letter one morning from an address in Paignton offering it to me and the letter described the car's colour and length. Most importantly, the writer told me that it had a trade mark which contained the letters GBN. This was sufficient to send me off to Devon at the earliest opportunity, and I was not disappointed when I arrived there. The car had been made in 1904 and was in perfect condition, painted white with pink lining and orange wheels and seats. It had four lamps and a luggage rack at the back. Originally it would have had a model chauffeur made of plaster and possibly three passengers too but none of these had survived. I was warned by the owner that the car would damage the furniture if it was wound up and left to run across the floor! Needless to say it would never suffer any such indignity and violence in my hands. In 1970s terms I offered a lot of money for the model and, as soon as I could safely stop on the way home, carefully examined the model car which was tucked away in its original box on the back seat to reassure myself that in my enthusiasm I hadn't paid far too much!

1904 Bing Mercedes Benz Tourer.

Bing boats

The paint on my 1920s three funnel Bing liner betrayed its age and, as it wasn't a toy of any great value, I undertook what work of restoration was desirable myself. Whenever such work is necessary the key is to do no more than is absolutely essential so the paintwork of the liner, when finished, remained mostly original. The ship was 50 cm long and of course lacked the presence of Bing's larger and much more impressive 100 cm model.

On one occasion I was able to buy a metre-long four-funnelled torpedo boat from before the First World War in two shades of grey with an enormous clockwork motor and key to match but, sadly, I have no photographs of it now.

There was also a very early Bing battleship made long before the First World War which, although two feet in length and heavy, had been allowed to become a child's bath toy. When all the soap and suds had been removed it was still in quite good shape.

1920s Bing clockwork liner.

An earlier liner of similar size was devoid of any paint so I really had no choice other than to repaint it entirely. The secret in such cases is to avoid absolute precision of line if one is to make it look at all convincing. But I was never happy with it.

I was once offered three Bing boats from an address in London and, as soon as I saw them, I realised they were the same ones that had been sold at the auction in Canterbury. Knowing precisely how much each had fetched at the auction I declined to pay what was being asked for them but offered instead the amounts that had been paid at the sale. Each had to be assessed individually and each was duly taken by its owner into an adjoining room where, I was told, his elderly parent's decision was sought. In each case my offer was accepted and I came away with all three boats.

1920s Bing liner much restored.

An 0 gauge fireball!

Bing's output was truly prodigious and at the other end of the scale from the gauge IV monsters the firm produced many inexpensive and simple 0 gauge trains of 0-4-0 configuration both in clockwork and steam. I decided one day to set my early 0 gauge Bing steamer going on a circle of rails on the study carpet and, filling the boiler with water and the burner with methylated spirits, put a match to it. The result was impressive as the tiny locomotive, pulling a tender and three four-wheeled carriages, gathered ever-increasing speed. Then disaster struck as the meths started to slop about and flames began to lick around and then on top of the boiler. The train became a fast moving ball of flame and threatened to set fire to the house after creating a circle of flames on the carpet. I rushed to the kitchen and returned with a bowlful of water which I threw over the blaze. Thankfully this extinguished the fire and stopped the train before too much damage had been done!

6
GEORGES CARETTE

GEORGES CARETTE WAS THE SON of a Parisian photographer, and he moved to Nuremberg when he came to live with the Hopfs who were the friends of his parents.

Herr Hopf, being impressed by the great interest Georges had shown in mechanical toys from the time he was a young boy, helped him to establish his own toy factory in 1886 at 5 Schillerstasse. To get himself started Carette set up a working relationship with Bing but eventually he became entirely independent and developed his own extensive range of toy cars, boats and trains which rivalled those of the other famous German toy manufacturers.

In 1893 Carette exhibited an electrically-driven model at the distant Columbia Exposition in America and a few years later Paul Josephstal came into his firm as a partner. As was the case with Bing, Carette made a business arrangement with Bassett-Lowke so that he produced models specifically for the British market which were also sold in the big London stores.

Although married to a German girl, George Carette, being a Frenchman naturally found it difficult to remain in Germany during the First World War and because of this returned to France to live in Paris. It was in Paris where he had been born that he died not long after the war. His factory closed at the height of the action in 1917.

Carette Trade Marks

1898-1904   1905-1917

40 cm Carette limousine

One of the most famous Carette toys to be made before the First World War is known as the Carette limousine. Loosely modelled on a large Mercedes Benz limousine of about 1908, Carette produced this model in different sizes and qualities and I came across my first one in a vicarage in deepest Dorset. It was an example of the largest of the lithographed cars and so was dark green in colour and measured 40 cm. It had four magnificent lamps, two in the front and two on the windscreen pillars, bevelled glass windows and a tinplate driver dressed in the uniform of a chauffeur. As one would have expected, the car was equipped with tinplate wheels and tyres. The incumbent of the parish had often amused the local schoolchildren by winding up the car's powerful clockwork motor and sending it speeding across the classroom floor, no doubt banging into the legs of desks, chairs and children on its way. Thankfully the venerable old model had survived this treatment with minimal damage to its lithographed bodywork and although the car's white tin tyres had become slightly discoloured with superficial rust it would have been a crime to repaint them. The whole car was in good original condition except for the fact that the handle was missing from one of its doors and a friend, who was an engineer and a railwayman, fabricated one in brass which was a perfect replica so that it was indistinguishable from the original door handle.

A large lithographed Carette limousine.

32 cm Carette limousine

My next Carette limousine was of medium size, being just 32 cm in length. It was unusual in that it was of intermediate quality, having a lithographed body and a tinplate driver but at the same time boasted cast metal wheels, which were enamelled cream and shod with white rubber tyres. In this size Carette limousines were equipped with only two lamps, one each side of the wind-screen, but this one had bevelled glass windows and was coloured a most attractive shade of grey lined in red and dark green. It had been lovingly cared for by the bank manager who had been its proud owner since he had been given it brand new when he was a boy. In my estimation it was the best looking of all the medium-sized lithographed Carette limousines, and it appeared with the others in David Pressland's *The Art of the Tin Toy*.

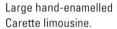

1908 Carette limousine.

40 cm and hand enamelled

The pride of my Carette collection was undoubtedly a large hand enamelled example of the limousine with a plaster driver. It was white with blue lining and had a pale blue roof and maroon seats. It had four large lamps and its pink cheeked chauffeur wore a dark blue uniform and looked ready to take milady to the theatre at any time.

The extra weight of the car's substantial body is exemplified by the extra support provided on each side for the running boards. It is arguably the finest toy car that anyone has ever made.

1906 Carette two-seater

I came across a lithographed open two-seater Carette car at an address in Birmingham. White with gold lining and black mudguards, it was 26 cm in length. Its wheels were cast metal painted red and it had white rubber tyres. Sadly its lamp brackets had been badly affected by rust and, to my horror, one of them, which had evidently been hanging on by a mere thread of rusted metal, came away in my hands as, with infinite care, I took the car from its owner. He was beside himself with sorrow and rage and just kept repeating that he couldn't understand how such a thing could have happened after the car had remained intact for so many years. It was rather like the scene with the Allard driver in the film "Genevieve". He seemed to imply that I might have deliberately broken the lamp bracket to reduce its value! In spite of this harsh and unjust accusation I felt a

Large hand-enamelled Carette limousine.

degree of sympathy for him in his anguish. It was as though he had regressed to being the five year old who had been given the car when it was new. It would have been of no use pointing out to him that the lamp bracket might have held on for another ten years if it had been allowed to remain totally undisturbed in his loft. Somehow I managed to assuage his wrath and left as soon as this could decently be achieved. In fact I restored the lamp bracket to the car very easily with the merest touch of Araldite but, what was much more difficult to rectify was the absence of the car's large tinplate driver. Lacking its driver, the car looked strangely empty and inadequate and I so fashioned a suitable figure for the vehicle out of clay. In his book, David Pressland wrote that the "the bowler hatted driver is not 1906 Carette but a 1974 Bryan Apps sculpture!"

1906 Carette No. 50

Strangely my next Carette car also came from Birmingham. The model was known as the No. 50 because that number appeared conspicuously on its front and back. The model was featured in *L'age d'or des Jouets* by J. Reise and J. Fondin and, for this reason I had been looking out for one for some time. Again, it was lithographed and rather fragile but it had an attractive metal canopy over its four seated occupants who consisted of two identical gentlemen in the front and two identical ladies in the back. Its two lamps were similar to those of the two-seater Carette car and not nearly as finely crafted as those on the limousines.

1906 Carette No. 50.

1904 gauge III live steam 4-4-0

My live steam Carette locomotive was a rare addition to my collection. It had a six-wheeled tender and was of Continental rather than British outline, being intended originally for the German market. It could not be claimed to represent any particular locomotive and was similar, although much more impressive in its general design, to the much more common 4-2-0 steam models which are popularly known as "storklegs." The fact that it was a large gauge III model made it very imposing indeed. Its boiler and outside cylinders were unpainted, as must always have been the case, and its body was dark green with red lining. One could only imagine what it would have looked and sounded like as it sped around a vast circle of 2.5 inch gauge rails. I wonder how many mansions were burnt to the ground by such great beasts getting out of hand!

Live steam Continental style gauge III 4-4-0 by Carette.

1904 gauge III live steam 4-2-0

Eventually one of the 2-2-0 Carette trains joined the collection and, being also built to gauge III and in perfect condition, made a good comparison with the one above.

Gauge III Stirling Single

In the 1897 edition of the Encyclopaedia Britannica there is a section on what was then the current design of steam locomotives and it explained how it had been well established that the most effective design for the fastest express trains was the 4-2-2 wheel arrangement known as the Single. It cited in particular the Great Northern Railway Stirling Single as being the last word in locomotive design, overlooking the advantage of the greater traction that coupled wheels would provide.

In the 1902 Bassett-Lowke catalogue the gauge III Stirling Single made by George Carette took pride of place. In the same catalogue the gauge III live steam LSWR 4-4-0 "Black Prince,"

Gauge III live-steam Carette 4-2-0 1902.

similar to my "King Edward" was listed at £3 15s 6d and the gauge IV version of my LSWR 4-4-0 steamer was £4 15s 6d. The Stirling Single, although 'only' gauge III, was priced at £6 6s 0d! Great attention to detail had been given by Carette in the design of this model with the characteristic splashers over its two great driving wheels and with smoke box sides that swept out and over the outside cylinders.

The following description appears of the model in the Bassett-Lowke catalogue.

"This Locomotive is built entirely of CASTINGS throughout and is fitted with a strong Brass Boiler, Double Action Slide-Valve Cylinders, fitted with Link Motion Reversing Gear worked by a lever in cab, 4 in. turned Brass driving wheels, exhaust steam into funnel, Steam Dome, Safety Valve, Whistle in cab, turned Brass Hand Rail, three Headlights, loose 4-wheel Bogie Carriage. The Tender is fitted with a Spirit Tank with Cock and Rubber Tube for supplying Spirit Lamp. The whole Locomotive, including the Boiler, is enamelled and finished in best style and in correct GNR colours, and in every small detail has had our careful attention. We can safely say it is the finest model of its kind on the market. This Locomotive is very powerful and will run for half-an-hour without stop. Length over all 24 in., Height. 7.75 in. Steam Gauge and Syphon 7/6 extra."

I bought an example of this extremely rare model at an auction at Sothebys in London and it was in exceptionally good condition. The paint on the boiler of live-steam models usually suffered greatly with use but in this case there was very little evidence of burning. The price at the auction rose much higher than its estimate but I was determined to secure it as I had recently agreed to loan my entire collection to Allen Levy's London Toy Museum which was soon to open and this would be one of the museum's prime exhibits. I would never have attempted to fire the model, having regard for the paintwork on its boiler but, in spite of Bassett-Lowke's claim that it was very powerful, its heavy cast metal parts must surely have slowed it down when attempting to pull a rake of gauge III carriages.

Gauge III Stirling Single.

7
THE MARKLIN BROTHERS

THEODOR FRIEDRICH WILHELM MARKLIN came to Goppingen in 1840 with the sole object of making toys. His first products were tinplate doll's pots, pans and cooking stoves and his wife Karoline travelled throughout Germany and Switzerland selling them. Sadly, Theodor died following an accident in 1866, and Karoline ran the business herself until her sons were old enough to take over as the Marklin Brothers in 1880.

The gifted brothers took one of their model railways to the Leipzig Trade Fair in 1891 with extra rails with which to make an impressive layout for the demonstration of their models. Four years later they had a larger factory built in Marketstrasse, Goppingen where, in addition to model trains, they manufactured tinplate boats and horse drawn carriages. Still larger premises were soon found to be necessary in 1900 and these were constructed in Stuttgarterstrasse, measuring 6,000 square metres.

In 1892 Emil Fiz joined the Marklin brothers as a partner and so the firm became Marklin Brothers & Company before an additional partner, Richard Safft joined them in 1908.

In 1911 Marklin moved into a new building with six floors and by this time its employees numbered six hundred. With the outbreak of the First World War Marklin acquired all the assets of Hornby in Germany but, as with other toy makers on each side of the Channel, all the firm's resources had to be directed to the war effort.

After the war Marklin quickly returned to the peaceful pursuit in which it excelled. Emil Fiz died in 1922 and his son-in-law, Max Scheerer became a director of the company in 1923. Eugen Marklin retired in 1930, and his son Fritz, who had joined the firm some years earlier, took his place.

In 1939 Marklin's energies were again applied to military purposes and after the War Herbert Safft, Richard's son, became the Managing Director. Fritz, the surviving member of the Marklin family, left the firm but its future was assured with a staff of two thousand.

Marklin became the longest surviving manufacturer of model trains in the world and no other toy manufacturer, with the possible exception of Hornby, has attracted such devoted admirers. In its earlier years Marklin showed less concern for accuracy of scale and line than Bing but this resulted in a certain distinctive charm becoming synonymous with Marklin designs which a greater degree of realism would have ruled out. The same charm is evident in all the early Marklin products which exude quality. Many were sold by Gamages with their own label and also by Harrods and Hamleys. As with the products of the other German manufacturers, Marklin locomotives accurately reproduced the liveries of all the pre-1923 English railway companies so they now provide the best available reference point in this respect for the restoration of full size locomotives of the period. A greater degree of freedom was possible with regard for the colour schemes of cars, railway stations and other items and in such cases Marklin possessed an inspired judgement.

Marklin Trade Marks

Pre-1914   Post-1918

A Marklin limousine

Pre-1914 Marklin cars are rarely found today and it creates a sensation amongst collectors when one does come to light. It seems that the days have long gone when people came across early toys in the attics of old houses but they turned up very occasionally in the early 1970s.

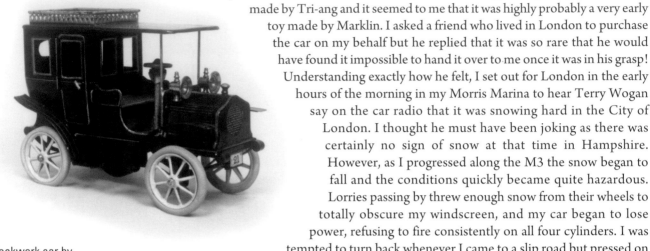

It was just before Christmas one year when a man phoned me from London to say that he had come across a toy car made of tin which was about the size of a Minic product of the 1930s. The description didn't suggest anything that was ever made by Tri-ang and it seemed to me that it was highly probably a very early toy made by Marklin. I asked a friend who lived in London to purchase the car on my behalf but he replied that it was so rare that he would have found it impossible to hand it over to me once it was in his grasp! Understanding exactly how he felt, I set out for London in the early hours of the morning in my Morris Marina to hear Terry Wogan say on the car radio that it was snowing hard in the City of London. I thought he must have been joking as there was certainly no sign of snow at that time in Hampshire. However, as I progressed along the M3 the snow began to fall and the conditions quickly became quite hazardous. Lorries passing by threw enough snow from their wheels to totally obscure my windscreen, and my car began to lose power, refusing to fire consistently on all four cylinders. I was tempted to turn back whenever I came to a slip road but pressed on regardless, never being able to better 30 miles per hour. Fortunately the weather situation improved as I arrived in London and I soon found the address where the toy car was to be seen. It had suffered in some respects over the years and was in need of expert restoration but its original paintwork was in exceptionally good condition. Above all it had indeed been made by Marklin and well before 1914. The best guess was that it was made in 1905 and I was delighted with my purchase. What restoration work that was required was carried out by Chris Littledale the most skilful of all restorers at his works in Brighton, and he told me that everyone who saw the car while it was in his hands desperately wanted to buy it from me. .

1909 clockwork car by Marklin.

That Marklin limousine, which is sadly no longer mine, was one of three sizes of clockwork cars that Marklin made and I considered it to be both the smallest and the best. Of course that opinion wouldn't have been shared by the owners of larger Marklin cars, but this one had an innocence and charm which the larger models lacked and when Justin Knowles of Denys Ingram published "Marklin 1895–1914" he devoted two whole pages to photographs of my find.

It was shown one Saturday in a television programme for children after I had loaned the car to the London Toy Museum. Where it is now I have no idea but I'm quite certain that it isn't lying hidden in an attic and gathering dust!

Marklin clockwork ship the Luzern.

The *Luzern*

One of my favourite toys was the *Luzern*, a two funnelled clockwork liner which was made by Marklin in the mid 1920s. It was only 35 cm long but, being made by Marklin, had the presence of a much larger vessel built by Bing or Carette. Hand-enamelled and clockwork powered, one of its masts was missing but, as it was entirely original in every other respect, I had no intention of having a second mast fabricated however well it might have been crafted. I floated the boat in a bath filled with water and even ventured it on our fishpond in the garden. It floated low in the water and, while making good progress when fully wound, excited the interest of the goldfish and newts.

The *Deutchland*

When I first saw the twin funnelled Marklin passenger liner *Deutchland*, which was made in about 1909, it had *Uruguay* emblazoned on either side of it bow. It was in a sorry state with its funnels, life boats, masts and rigging all stowed away below decks after its long journey from South America where it had been chanced upon by a doll collector. I had agreed to buy it unseen to enable the purchase of some dolls to be completed on the other side of the Atlantic. All the impor-

tant bits were there but the whole ship was in urgent need of expert care and attention. By Marklin's standards it was a medium sized ship, 72 cm or 28.25 in long, and it promised to be quite splendid after being professionally restored. It was obvious that the ship's paint was in generally good condition, including the important planked decking and the portholes painted on the sides of the hull. However it soon became apparent that the name *Uruguay* was not original and had probably been applied after the model had left the shores of Germany. With careful restoration, the original name *Deutchland* was revealed beneath. I painted a company flag appropriately and was pleased to receive the model back, looking ship shape once more. In "Marklin 1995 – 1914" there is a two page spread of *Carmania* which is an identical model but named and painted by Marklin for the British market. I wondered whether the *Deutchland* may have been hastily removed from Germany and taken to South America by its owner after the Second World War.

Marklin steam ship the 'Deutchland'.

A 1906 gauge II Marklin train set

When offered an old 0 gauge clockwork Hornby train set through an advertisement in a local paper I was surprised to discover that it had in fact been made by Marklin in gauge II in about 1906. It was complete with its original box which had an attractive picture of a terminus station on its lid. It was a simple 0-4-0 locomotive with a four wheel tender of typical early Marklin design. The four wheeled coaches and wagons were what one might have expected of a gauge I set but it was much more impressive in gauge II. The whole set was completely original and in remarkably good condition.

An early Marklin station

The young man who later brought to me a tinplate railway station was delighted to learn that it was made by Marklin, possibly as early as 1904 instead of being a much later station by Hornby. It was made for gauge I along the lines of the famous Gare d'Orsay in Paris and was very attractively hand enamelled. It was the perfect complement to my two gauge I Marklin trains of the same period.

A gauge I 0-2-2 Marklin train

The 0-2-2 locomotive could have been made as early as 1895, being modelled, with a great deal of artistic licence upon one of the 4-2-2 Single locomotives which were designed for maximum

Gauge 1 Marklin 0-2-2 train with early Marklin station.

Complete Marklin gauge II train set with its box.

speed. The four wheeled tender and coaches were typical of the period prior to the First World War and it was a really charming set.

A gauge I 0-4-0 Marklin GNR set

The GNR Marklin train.

The Great Northern Railway 0-4-0 locomotive was extremely rare even in terms of Pre 1914 Marklin toys. Possibly made especially for Harrods, it was a very free representation of what might have been a 2-4-0 or 4-4-0 design in real life but it had been given an English feel about the cab and the splashers. The two coaches were also highly unusual, being hand enamelled in GNR brown and extending beyond the enclosed carriages at the front and the back. Inside the passengers were afforded the luxury of cloth covered seats with spikes to hold them uncomfortably in place as the train negotiated the sharp curves. Brass fittings on the locomotive added to the general effect.

A Pre 1914 blue Marklin carriage

Marklin carriage.

It had no trade mark but such was the quality of the quite small but attractive closed carriage, which was hand enamelled in blue and black with red wheels, that it could only have been made by Marklin. It was an early example and had been preserved in beautiful condition, complete with its two fine lamps. Sadly the horse had been lost.

A large open carriage by Marklin

The open carriage was built by Marklin on a massive scale, as can be seen when compared to the gauge II Marklin locomotive alongside it. The body of the carriage was black, its wheels and detailed undercarriage yellow, and seats blue. The magnificent horse was also made

by Marklin and, with the carriage, echoed a more gracious age far removed from our own. It is possibly one of the very earliest designs of the Marklin brothers.

The largest Marklin horse and carriage with a gauge II Marklin loco.

A Marklin look-alike closed brougham

The maker of the closed carriage and tinplate horse has not been identified but, while it was certainly not made by Marklin, it is similar and from the same period as the one above. More probably made in France than Germany, it is beautifully proportioned and the interior has cloth upholstery in red. Its original owner was said to have occupied a senior position in one of the big Banks in the City of London and, I was told, had become Lord Mayor of London. When the model first came into my hands the original finish had been over painted, and even though this had been carefully executed, it detracted from its interest and value as an antique toy. Fortunately I discovered that by rubbing it gently with clear wax polish on a soft cloth the outer layer of paint gradually came away, leaving the original enamel, complete with its yellow lines, in sparking condition.

The closed brougham.

8
SOME LESSER LIGHTS

Wendy with the red Gunthermann car bought at Canterbury.

Large Gunthermann 'Vis a Vis', 1900.

Rear view of the Gunthermann car.

FOLLOWING THE CHAPTERS ON BING, CARETTE AND MARKLIN, I describe the toy makers that follow as being lesser lights only in the sense that the stars are lesser lights than the sun. All are worthy of their place in this book in the company of their more august peers.

Gunthermann

Siegfried Gunthermann founded his toy making business in Nuremberg in 1887 and, after he died his widow married his company's manager, Adolf Weigel. This accounts for the Guthermann trademark bearing the initials AW from 1903 to 1920. Gunthermann made a number of interesting toys, the best known of which was the "Vis a Vis" car in its various sizes, but Gunthermann was never quite in the same league as the three mentioned above.

The firm was taken over by Siemens in 1965.

H. Fischer & Co

H. Fischer and Company was founded in 1908 and most of its toys had a figure dressed in armour or a fish as its trademark. The Express Parcels Delivery lorry must have been quite inexpensive,

being made of thin tin and lithographed, but it has a lot going for it with its canvas cover, tin plate driver, and well proportioned lines.

Bub

Karl Bub produced toys, largely in collaboration with Carette and Issayer in the earlier years from 1851. His first clockwork trains date from 1903 and when the production of Bing models came to an end in 1932 Bub took over his former rival's tooling. Bub model locomotives were at the cheaper end of the market and thin sheets of metal were used in their production. They were sold in America through Schwartz in New York. The Bub factory was destroyed during the Second World War but production was able to be resumed afterwards and continued until 1966.

1910 Express Parcel's Delivery lorry by H. Fischer & Co.

0 Gauge Bub locomotive and carriage.

Chad Valley

Anthony Bunn Johnson established a small printing and book binding business in Birmingham early on in the nineteenth century, and in 1860 his sons Joseph and Alfred set out on their own as printers and book binders in George Street in Birmingham, calling their business Messrs Johnson Bros. Thirty-seven years later they moved to Harborne and called their factory the Chad Valley Works, naming it after an adjoining stream. From manufacturing items of stationery they diversified into board games and toys and this eventually led to Chad Valley becoming the largest toy manufacturer in the land.

Joseph Johnson died in 1904 and his eldest son Alfred became Chad Valley's chairman and managing director. His brothers, Arthur and Harry joined him and also Ephraim Dent who, after long service in the company, became its managing director in 1932.

In the absence of any imported toys during the First World War Chad Valley produced a range of Teddy Bears and, in 1916 patented a machine for stuffing them. In 1919 the Harborne Village Institute was purchased and used for the manufacture of packaging for Chad Valley's products. A new factory was built in Wellington in Shropshire, known as the Wrekin Toy Works and began to make teddy bears the following year.

Tinplate blacksmith c1904, maker unkown.

Chad Valley bears can be identified by their celluloid covered buttons with the words "Hygienic Toys made in England by Chad Valley Co. Ltd" imprinted on them, and the woven labels with the same words embroidered in red before 1938 when the Royal warrant was granted to them and in blue afterwards.

The Chad Valley Company Limited, as it came to be called, continued to grow so that a new factory was completed in Harborne in 1932 with six floors and it produced a range of teddy bears in fourteen different sizes. Peacock and Company was acquired and Chad Valley added dolls and wooden toys to its output.

From 1930 a great many wooden jigsaw puzzles were made by Chad Valley including the famous range of the Great Western Railway,

Then in 1938 the Chad Valley Company was granted the Royal Warrant as both princesses played with Chad Valley toys.

Earliest known toy of a working mechanical road vehicle c1900.

Chad Valley dolls at Harrods
before the war.
Courtesy Company Archive Harrods
Limited

Inevitably the resources of Chad Valley were directed towards the war effort from 1939 until 1945 when it produced, amongst other things, barrels for anti aircraft guns and hospital tables.

In 1946 an additional factory was built in Wellington for the manufacture of rubber toys and, in the years that followed the company acquired Hall and Lane Limited, Roberts Bros Limited, the Acme Stopper and Box Company Limited and H. G. Stone and Company Limited and at this point, in the late 1950s, it became the largest manufacturer of toys in this country.

After this, with the takeover by John Bentley, the writing was on the wall for Chad Valley. Having also acquired Tri-ang Pedigree, Bentley closed the Harborne factory and made half of its employees redundant. In the early seventies he closed two more factories and then proceeded to sell the company. Only two factories remained in 1975 and the company was bought by Palitoy in 1978. The Hall and Lane factory was closed in 1979 and the name of Chad Valley was acquired by Woolworth in 1988, which would itself go in to liquidation twenty years later.

In happier times Chad Valley manufactured Winnie the Pooh bears in the 1950s and acquired the exclusive right to make Harry Corbet's television favourites Sooty and Sweep. Sadly Chad Valley is no more.

Lehmann

Lehmann 'Tut Tut'.

Ernst Paul Lehmann established a toy factory in Brandenburg in 1880 and produced a range of inexpensive tinplate toys. Amongst his most popular products was the Tut Tut car which had a large figure of a man who blew a horn. Another mechanical toy took the form of a father who slaps at his "naughty boy" as he sits in the front seat of his car. Lehmann's toys were often whimsical, one being of a monkey climbing a pole. Ernst died in 1934 and his cousin Johannes Richter succeeded him in the business. He was responsible for the ingenious Skirolf skier. The East German Government took control of the company in 1948 but Richter moved to Nuremberg in West Germany and he continued with the business there.

L.G.B.

In 1968 Richter's sons, Eberhard and Wolfgang, produced L.G.B. which stands for Lehmann Gross Bahn, or Lehmann's Big Train. They were made to G scale, four times the scale of H0 and their first model was of the 0-4-0 Austrian locomotive "Stairz" which was given a circular track of four foot diameter. L.G.B. is ideal for a garden railway being extremely strong and relatively inexpensive. When I first moved to Bournemouth in 1978 I built a railway in the back garden of my vicarage, with layers of roof tiles cemented together to make a substantial base for the track which passed around a fishpond at its further end. There was an L.G.B. station and other buildings which I stored indoors when the railway was not in use. When the large Crocodile locomotive pulled six bogie coaches around the track it both looked and sounded most impressive. I had several locomotives and assorted coaches and wagons and also two L.G.B trams of different designs. I finally

LGB garden railway.

LGB garden railway.

LGB Zillertal.

parted with it all when I had insufficient time to maintain the track adequately. Eventually L.G.B. was led by the two brother's sons, Johnannes and Rolf and in recent years it was acquired by Marklin. It seems that L.G.B. must reached its zenith at the time that I had my garden railway. The entire L.G.B. range was available at Hamleys one Christmas including the limited edition and highly expensive models. I understand that its range of models has been greatly reduced since.

THE LONDON STORES

I T WOULD BE DIFFICULT to overestimate the importance of the big London stores, and the little shop at 112 High Holborn, in the development of toys and models for the British market towards the end of the nineteenth century and in the early years of the twentieth century. Hamleys, Gamages and Harrods together with Bassett-Lowke, were able to place orders of sufficient magnitude to be able to meet the exacting requirements of their discerning customers.

Christmas lights in London, 2009.

9
HAMLEYS OF REGENT STREET

WILLIAM HAMLEY CAME FROM BODMIN in Cornwall to open a toy shop in Holborn in 1760, long before the arrival of motor transport and at a time when only horses, carts and pedestrians crossed Westminster Bridge. He called his shop Noah's ark and sold a wide range of toys, including rag dolls, tin soldiers, hoops and wooden horses. Determined to make his shop the finest in the world, he described it as a "'Joy Emporium", The shop at 231 Holborn was destroyed by fire in 1901 and afterwards it reopened at numbers 86 and 87 in the same road. William's grandsons moved the store to its present site at 188 to 196 Regents Street near Piccadilly Circus in 1881, before the arrival of Eros. Jean Jacques launched 'Gossima' in 1891 exclusively through Hamleys and in 1921 it became better known as table tennis, not just a popular pastime but a serious competitive sport. Hamleys was then the largest toy shop in the world, selling toy theatres, puppets and model railways.

In 1931 the shop was bought by Walter Lines of Lines Bros and Tri-ang fame, and in 1938 Queen Mary, granted it a Royal Warrant as it was from Hamleys that she

Hamleys today.

A rare Gossima set from the nineteenth century.

51

had purchased toys and dolls for her granddaughters. During the Second World War Hamleys was bombed five times and at one point the staff wore helmets as they dashed in and out with toys for their customers to purchase outside on the pavement, everyone responding to the emergency in true London style.

At the Festival of Britain in 1951 Hamleys was commissioned to provide a great model railway and a display of dolls, and in 1955 a second Royal Warrant was issued to the shop by Queen Elizabeth II as a Toy and Sports Merchant.

Hamleys, which became a public company in 1994, occupies 54,000 square metres on seven floors. Lego, for example, is to be found in the basement, while soft toys are always on the ground floor. Board games are on the first floor and toys for pre-school children on the second. Dolls, and other toys for girls are on the third floor and boys' toys, such as model railways, including the latest offerings from Bassett-Lowke, and Scalextric on the fourth. Finally, on the top floor there are diecast models, action figures, and a cafe which is very welcome to weary parents and grandparents. The Store continues to be packed with shoppers of all ages on its seven floors, especially in the weeks before Christmas.

I am grateful to Gudjon Reynisson and Maria de Oliveira his Office Manager and PA for providing me with some pages from some of Hamleys' earlier catalogues for this book.

Early large-scale toy Hamleys Lorry by Tri-ang.

Hamleys

▶ **SRI steamroller**

The first live moving steam model first manufactured nearly 40 years ago and still going strong. Made in Birmingham this attractive looking model is made primarily from steel and brass.

8135   £99.99

Age 14+

▲ **Flying Scotsman**

The LNER Class A1 4-6-2 locomotive and classic teak coaches in this Hornby electric trainset depict the Flying Scotsman as it ran non-stop from London to Edinburgh in the 1930's.

This set includes the starter oval track plus the extension track packs A and B to form a layout with two sidings (additional track packs can also be bought to enlarge it). Comes complete with locomotive, two composite coaches, one brake composite coach, buffer stops, wall plug transformer, train controller, power connecting clip and trackmat(r). Track 164cm (65in) x 94cm (37in).

419820   £99.99

Age 5+

▼ **LGB railway**

An easy to assemble electronic train set including a Stainz steam locomotive with a powerful Buhler motor, electronic sound featuring authentic steam train noises and a smoke generator for realistic effects. In additioin ther are two colourful passenger coaches, five action figures, a full circle of track (130cm diameter) with quick connect cable and a powerful 1 amp power pack. Suitable for outdoor use.

563502   £179.99

Age 3+

HAMLEYS COLLECTION

A
TIN BUS
Replica of old brass model. By Mamod.
8 years +. **£184.00**

B
TIN VAN
Replica of old brass model. By Mamod.
8 years +. **£99.99**

C
LONDON BUS
Die-cast reproduction model of the double decker. By Corgi.
4 years +. **£5.50**

D
LONDON TAXI
Die-cast model with accurate detail.
By Corgi.
4 years +. **£5.50**

E
BRITISH RAIL CLASSIC SET
Limited Edition of 10,000 worldwide die-cast delivery van sets.
By Corgi.
4 years +. **£22.39**

F
9th NOVEMBER BERLIN WALL
Limited Edition of 1,000 'The Symbol of Freedom'. A piece of the West Wall, barbed wire from the East and an East German car. By SES.
S *8 years+.* **£19.99**

Hamleys exclusive die-cast replica models all with hand-painted detail. By Lledo.

G
TROLLEY BUS
£3.99

H
MODEL A VAN
£3.99

I
MOCK CANVAS BACK VAN £3.99

J
MORRIS VAN
£3.99

10
GAMAGES OF HOLBORN

ARTHUR WALTER GAMAGE was the son of a Herefordshire farmer, but when he came to London he was apprenticed to a draper. He showed great enterprise and business acumen when, in 1878 at the age of twenty-one, he leased a small shop with a frontage of only five feet in Holborn with Frank Spain. Displaying in large letters on his shop front the words "Tall oaks from little acorns grow," he proceeded to prove the point emphatically in the years that followed. He and Spain slept in the back room of the shop and set out to undercut the prices of all their competitors. The word soon got round and in 1881 Arthur Gamage bought his partner's share of the business for £425 when Spain, having become engaged to be married, decided that he should settle for a less risky future for himself and his wife. After this Arthur began to buy one by one the equally small shops on either side of his shop so that by 1890 he owned most of the properties between Leather Lane and Hatton Gardens. In this way the greatly enlarged store began to assume its unique character, being composed of a vast number of small rooms joined by short passages which were interrelated but on different levels so that the customers were constantly going up or down steps or ramps as they went from one room to another. Those who flocked to the shop found it to be an adventure to navigate its interior in search of bargains. The enlarged Gamages became known as the "People's Popular Emporium" and, in addition to toys, sold books, shoes, furniture, jewellery, clothes, musical instruments, bicycles, cars and many more items too numerous to list. Arthur Gamage had a great fleet of Express Motor Vans offering free local delivery for items which cost more than 5 shillings, and he provided free postage to more distant addresses for items over £2. Liquids, ammunition, calcium carbide, rubber solution, fireworks and any explosives could not be sent by post! Gamages also proudly proclaimed that it was the official Scouts' outfitter and, no matter how eccentric the interior layout might have appeared to confused customers, the vast exterior of the store was palatial. Walter Gamage travelled far and wide in search of stock right across Europe and in the United States and, as a result of meeting Margarete Steiff in Germany, he became the biggest importer of her teddy bears and other stuffed animals. He also came upon the toy makers of Nuremberg and had a plentiful supply of tinplate cars, boats and trains. It could be claimed that Gamage established the world's first Super Market as he bought in bulk and sold as cheaply as possible to the widest range of customers. It must have been a memorable experience to enter the rabbit warren of rooms and passages that lay concealed behind the noble façade of his mega store.

It has been claimed that when Walter Gamage died in 1930 his body lay in state in the bicycle department with a guard of honour composed of the members of his staff, and no one would be at all surprised if that was indeed the case.

The Gamages store closed in 1972 and, sadly, its site was redeveloped.

BRITISH ARMOURED CRUISERS.

Modern Type, with 4 Funnels, and complete set of large and small guns.   Best make and finish.

Accurate Details in every respect, bridge, lifeboats, etc., good outlines.

155 441.	New Armoured Cruiser, driven by clockwork, 17 in. long			..	..	..	..	..	..	..	**10 9**
,, '442	..	..	,,	,,	21½ in. long with 2 lifeboats	..	..	..	..	**16 6**
,, '444	,,	..	,,	,,	29½ in. ,, 2 ,,	..	..	..	..	**22 6**
,, '445	..	,,	,,	..	33½ in. ,, 4 ,,	..	..	..	..	**45/-**
,, '446	..	,,	,,	..	37¼ in. ,, 4 ,,	..	..	..	..	**55/-**

Fine Model Liner "OLYMPIC" Type.

STRONGLY MADE AND BEAUTIFULLY ENAMELLED.

Fitted with finest clockwork mechanism.   A portion of deck can be removed at a moment's notice for oiling or inspecting works.

No. 0	16½ in. long, without lifeboats	..	**11/6**	Post 7d.	No. 2.	25½ in. long, with 4 lifeboats	..	**25/6**	Carriage free.
No. 1.	,, ,, ..	..	**15/-**	,, 9d.	No. 3.	32½ in. long, with 6 lifeboats	..	**45/-**	,,

No. 4. 30½ in. long with 10 lifeboats .. **65/-** Carriage free.

Superior Clockwork Fire Engines, etc.

Clockwork Motor Fire Engine (as illustration, with imitation rubber tyre and hose. Price . . **10½d.** Post 3d.

Clockwork Fire Escape (as illustration), with removable Ladders and Hose Pipe. Price **3 11** Post 5d.

Clockwork Fire Engine With Rubber Wheels. Price **2/11**

Latest Type Motor Fire Engine. Superior finish. Superior clockwork movement, fitted with change over gear, which will either run car or work the pump with water reservoir, complete pump gear, hose, bell, rubber tyres, front axle adjustable for straight or circular runs, fitted with brake, bell rings when running. 12 in. long. 4½ in. wide. 6½ in. high. **16/6** Post 6d.

Fine Model Clockwork Fire Engine. Hand fitted with brass boiler and head light, india rubber tyres. Fitted Automatic Pump, as illustration. Price . . **11/6** Post

Clockwork Steam Roller (as illustration. Runs forward and backwards. Price . . **10½d.** Post 3d.

Fine Model Clockwork Carpet Locomotive Price . . . . **3/11** Post 4d. Ditto, smaller and without cylinder. Price **10½d.** Post Larger . . **1/10½d.** Post 4d. Ditto, with tender. Price . . **2/6** Post 4d.

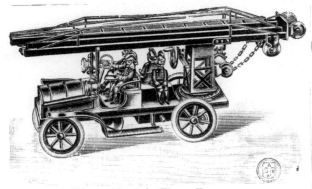

Fine Model Fire Escape. Ladder 34 in. high. Price . . **5/11** Post 4d.

Clockwork Model Fire Escape Fitted with Automatic Movement Ladder 3 Price . Post

GAMAGES OF HOLBORN   — 90 —   **BENETFINKS OF CHEAPSIDE.**

Superior Motor Cars and Lorries.

Clockwork Motor Bus in fine polychrome japanning, with strong clockwork. 12¾ in. long. 6¼ in. wide, with driver.
Price .. **2/11**   Post 3d.

Extraordinary Value, A complete Motor Garage with doors to o and 2 clockwork Motor Cars, exactly as illustration   **1/-**   Post 3d.

Limousine Motor Car. Strong clockwork movement, will run forward and backwards, also stop by lever in cab, can run straight or circular Length 12 in. Height 4½ in. Wide 5¾ in. Price **13 6**   Post 6d.

New Model Broughams. Torpedo bodies, strong clockwork me ment, rubber tyres, doors to open, fitted with brake, Bevel Glass Wind front axle adjustable to straight or circular run.
No. 3.   16 in. long, 6½ in. wide   ..   price, **25/-**
„ 4.   18½ „   7 „   ..   „ **35/-**

New Model Open Touring Car. Torpedo bodies, superior quality best hand-painted, strong, powerful clockwork movement, nicely regulated, rubber tyres, correct pattern seat, with brake, front axle adjustable for straight or circular run.   No. 1, 12½ in. long, 5½ in. wide ... **11/9** Post 6d.
No. 2, 15½ in. long, 6¼ wide   **21/-**

New Model Broughams. Torpedo bodies, superior qua strong clockwork movement with brake and rubber tyres, doors to Bevel Glass windows, front axle adjustable for straight or circular
No. 1.   10½ in. long, 4½ in. wide, price **8/11**   Post 4d.
„ 2.   13 „   5¼ „   „ **14 6**   „ 5d.

Motor Lorry with Tip-Up Body. Can be tilted as illustration. Superior quality and finish, strong clockwork movement, rubber tyres, front axle adjustable to allow either straight or circular run. 11¾ in. long, 3½ in. wide .. **5/11**   Post 4d.

Motor Lorry. Loaded with sacks, and covered with tarpa Very realistic. Strong clockwork movement.
8¼ in. long, 3½ in. wide   ..   ..   price **2 11**   Post

11
HARRODS OF KNIGHTSBRIDGE

CHARLES HENRY HARROD was a grocery wholesaler and tea merchant in Stepney but bought a small shop in Knightsbridge in 1849 when he foresaw the extra trade that would be generated by the Great Exhibition in 1851. In contrast to Gamages, Harrod and his son sought from the beginning to emphasise quality and service rather than affordability, and quickly gained a reputation for excellence. The store was destroyed by a fire in 1883 but rebuilt on the same site in a remarkably short time. Harrod established a company in 1889, by which time his store employed a staff of 200 and offered food, furniture, perfume, jewellery, and glass. In 1902 the first part of the Brompton Road frontage was completed and Harrods then had ninety-one departments. The Harrods slogan became "Everything for Everybody Everywhere." At the same time it remained a fashionable store for the more affluent customers. It was described at the time as one of the few smart rendezvous acknowledged and patronised by Society. By 1911 the purchase of all the surrounding properties had been completed and Harrods had become the first store in Britain to have an escalator. Having grown outwards, Harrods also grew upwards, converting store rooms for the sale of its goods.

Harrods in 2009.

In the 1970s I came across a 90 cm long Marklin Nassau class battleship which had been purchased from Harrod's in the early 1920s. It was a near scale model and its massive clockwork motor powered three propellers. Bristling with guns, cranes, searchlights, funnels and anchors, it represented that best that money could buy.

Harrods Annual Toy Fair became the venue to which all visitors to London, with or without children, would find their way. Oscar Wilde and Lilly Langtry were numbered amongst its customers and A. A. Milne purchased the original Winnie the Pooh there for his son Christopher.

Harrods once more came under private ownership when Mr Al Fayed purchased the store in 1985. I gave him a leaflet which had been issued by Harrods before the Christmas of 1905 which I had found in an old encyclopaedia. The leaflet was beautifully illustrated and contained a long list of members of the aristocracy who supported its annual Charity Appeal and it was added to the store's archives. I am grateful to Mr Al Fayed for allowing me to have access to the Harrods Archives through Sebastian Wormell his Archivist in compiling this book. Harrods is a great British institution to which the present owner has brought a distinctly Egyptian influence and it continues to flourish today, now under new ownership.

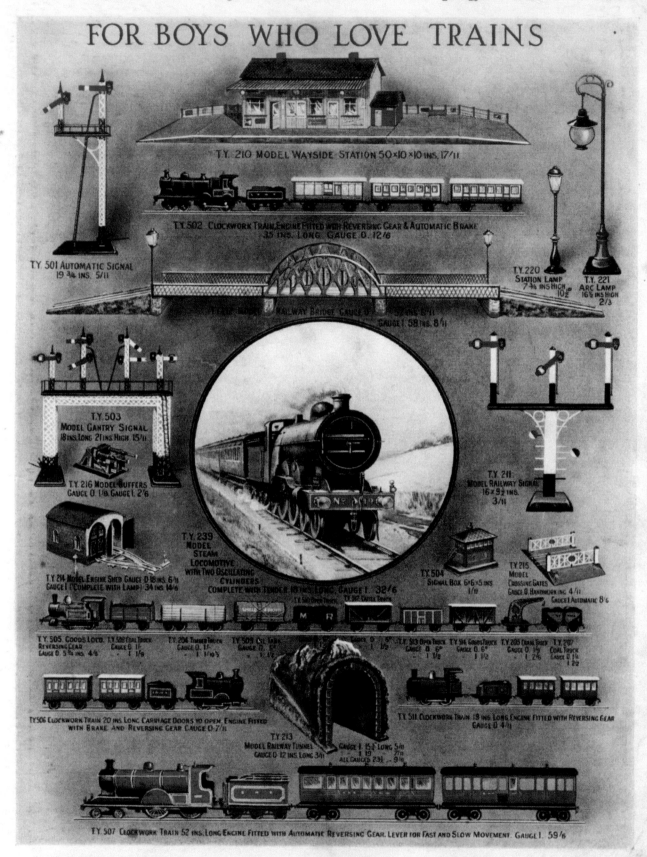

Marklin trains in the Harrods
catalogue of 1910.

Doll, doll's houses, prams and cots
in the Harrods catalogue of 1910.

Courtesy Company Archive Harrods Limited

The Harrods toy fair of 1929.
Courtesy Company Archive Harrods Limited

A Peep into Harrods Toy Fair

SUPPLEMENT TO HARRODS NEWS   NOVEMBER 18th, 1929

THE Fun of the Fair and all the joys
Of hundreds and thousands of lovely toys.
Bicycles, tricycles, motor-cars too,
All the things Daddy has—come, and walk through.
A party for dolls in a garden you'll see.
Fishing, and meeting their friends for tea.
A gigantic Noah's Ark at the end of the Hall
With hundreds of 'two's,' some large and some small.
Elephants, tigers, wool bears and Pekes
And birds with shoes and most marvellous beaks.
There's Tiger Tim and the bright Bruin Boys
And trumpets which make the loveliest noise.
There's 'Punch and Judy' and frogs which float,
A sieve and sand shapes made into a boat.
And a Zoo with animals in their cages—
Strong ones for lions in nasty rages.
Ask mummies and daddies to take you there
To HARRODS most wonderful GREAT TOY FAIR.

Neddy & Peke

A Peke is such a fussy dog,
He's careful whom he knows.
But see him talk to Neddy,
It's 'cos he's pink I s'pose.

Peke 6/6 & 8/11

Donkey 9/6, 12/- & 18/11

HARRODS CHRISTMAS STOCKINGS!

Filled with the most exciting things—gifts you would never dream of finding in stockings! They must not be mentioned here, of course, for 'Things in Stockings' always have to be kept a secret. But one thing *can* be said, and that is, you will be sure to love every present that comes out of them !

From 1/- *to* 12/11

My Seaplane

Here's the latest make of seaplane,
See her resting on her floats.
If you wind up her propellers
She will beat the fastest boats.

27/6

Won't you be Friends?

Can't we come and play with you?
I am Peter ; this is Prue.
I've a suit just like your own.
Prue is like your sister Joan.
We're so lonely, just us two,
Can't we come and play with you?

Each 27/6

Ride-a-Cock-Horse

My rocking horse has spots so gay
And the handsomest tail and mane.
Teddy and I go rides on his back
To there and back again.

60/-

Dinkie & Blinkie

Says 'Dinkie' Dog to 'Blinkie' Cat
" We're rather smart, you know.
" My purple nose is pretty and your
whiskers are like snow.
" My studded collar, too, is neat ;
in fact we're sure to please.
" I fancy we'll appear this year on
lots of Christmas trees."

Dog 8/9   *Cat* 10/11

At Harrods Toy Fair—You'll See us there!

Cuddly Bear

*A Cuddly Bear's a lovely toy to take to
bed at night;*
*He gives a little loving squeak each time
you hug him tight.*

6/11, 9/11, 12/11

BUILDING TOYS

Making things, is the nicest kind of
game and much the most exciting,
At Harrods there are hundreds of things
to make, and so many kinds of things
to make them with. Bricks, with which
you can build really proper looking
houses, pieces of wood which make the
most lovely toys—not to mention
Meccano and all those building toys
which are similar, and which you may
prefer if you are not very old.

Meccano 3/6 to £19.10.0
Various, from 3/6 to 42/-

Hans and Gretchen

*Little Dutch Girl, and little
Dutch Boy;*
He looks saucy; she looks coy.
*Little wooden shoes go clack!
clack! clack!*
*As they go for a walk to the town
and back.*

Each 25/6

Cock-a-Doodle-Doo!

*These cockerels will rock you
Fast or slow, high or low, to and fro.
They'll rock you at morning,
they'll rock you at noon;
Right up to the sun and right up to
the moon.*

34/6

A Thrilling Race

*Pedal! Pedal! legs fly round!
Who will win the race?
I think Jimmy Rabbit will
See his earnest face.*

Monkey 15/9   Rabbit 6/9
Dog 12/9

Who Goes There?

*The enemy is awfully fierce and cunning
as can be,
But our Fort will prove too strong for
them, as anyone can see.
We'll simply pull the drawbridge up
and as they climb the rocks
We'll shoot a hail of arrows that will
give them nasty shocks.*

13/11, 17/11, 23/6, 49/6 & 66/-

Quack! Quack!

*This is a very lazy duck.
He doesn't mind a swim,
But when he leaves the water,
He has wheels to carry him.*

6/-

The Golden Arrow

*You've heard of the Golden Arrow, the car that won the prize,
Well, here is one just like it, only made a nursery size.
It will go in half a second from London to Malay,
And even nurse will have to jump to get out of the way.*

8/11 and 16/6

The Harrods toy fair of 1929.
Courtesy Company Archive Harrods
Limited

Millions of Toys for Girls and Boys!

I want a Mummie!

Hush-a-bye baby! Aren't you real?
Little soft fingers seem to feel.
Real baby clothes and woolly shoes
There on her pillow she lies and coos.

53/6

Gee Up Dobbin!

Sweep up the leaves! Tidy and trim!
Here is a cart to put them in.
It's drawn by a horse whose name is Tim.
Don't you admire his glossy skin

49/6 and 65/-

And, Oh he Barks!

Now here's a dog who can walk and
bark.
(Keep cats right out of his way)
He'll go with you and Tim to the park,
He's not a bit afraid of the dark,
He is up to any old kind of lark
At any hour of the day.

9/6

DOLLIES' FURNITURE

There are sets of furniture for every kind of Dolly. Tiny dollies—dollies you carry—the kind that are rather large—and those as big as you. There are chairs and tables and beds and wardrobes—everything your dollies could possibly need. It is quite certain, that if you bring them to the Toy Fair, they are *sure* to want their houses refurnished.

For Dolls' Houses,
3/9, 5/9, 6/9 and 12/-
Larger Furniture,
12/6, 19/11, 21/-, 23/6
Child Size, 69/6 to 82/6

Moo! Moo!

" Moo!" says the Cow. " How d'ye do?" that's to say.
" I've a stool for my milking, a rack for my hay.
" My stable so cosy for when I feel dozy,
" And in between meals I go walks on my wheels."

12/-

FUN FOR PARTIES

You can have no end of fun at your party with the 'Surprises' which you can get at Harrods. No wonder they are so jolly, for who would think Toys could be made into a cake, a pie or a drum?

No one would think the snow-balls on the table had hats in them. And think how lovely it would be to open a pillar-box, a snow man or a chimney and find presents for girls and boys inside. And, just think! You could have a Lucky Tub for 'Dips.'

' Surprise' Snowballs, Pies, Pillar-boxes Chimneys, etc. From 4/- to 13/6

Carnival Novelties, 3d to 1/-

Hats from 2d. to 1/11

Now for a Joy Ride

My motor car's like Daddy's, of a
most superior build,
There's a luggage grid and dickey
(with my animals it's filled),
A windscreen and a buffer, and I
needn't even turn
When lighting up time comes, because
my headlights really burn.

£10 15 0
Other models from 15/- to £17 5 0

The Little Mother

When I take Dolly out to air
Other 'mothers' stop and stare.
They all wish that they had got
A pram that also is a cot.

20/-

For Fun by the Sea

Here goes a boat with a spade for sail
And wheels to use on land.
We'll take her down to the yellow
shore
And fill her up with sand.

8/11

A Peep into Harrods Toy Fair

Monkeys in Hat Box

What's in this hat box? Let's peep
  and see !
Two little monkeys, snug as can be ;
Pyjamas for each and a blanket and bow
I'm sure they'll be welcome wherever
  they go.

15/11

See my Shoes !

Mr. Penguin looks surprised,
A trifle jealous, too,
The little duck has shoes to wear,
Indeed, that's something new !

Penguin 3/11   Bird 3/6

A Lonely Bunny

I'm a little yellow rabbit
But I'm feeling rather blue.
I'm very lonesome on my own,
Can't I belong to you ?

6/-

KIDDIES' CYCLES

You would think you had wings if you
were to fly along on the Fairy Cycle
called ' Blue Bird.' This goes so beautifully because it has all those proper
things a bicycle *should* have. It would
take you all the way there and back
again in no time if you had one like it.

Blue Bird Cycles, 63/- to 78/6
Marmot Cycles 75/-
Fairy Cycles from 30/6 to 70/-

I Wheel my Wheelbarrow

Here I come with my wheelbarrow
Though the path is rather narrow,
If with dead leaves you will fill it
I'll be careful not to spill it.

13/-

TOY TOWN TRAINS

You will love to see the Trains at the
Toy Fair. They are going the whole
time—through tunnels, past stations—
stopping for signals — whirling away
through the country, by farms, villages
and towns. But you will make yours go
straight to the seaside that is certain.

Hornby Trains 6/- to 95/-
Various other makes 1/11 to 25/-

Tunnel 7/6

The Toy Fair is on
Harrods First Floor

To Water my Flowers

You can fill this pump with water
And push it round the paths,
And give the flowers and vegetables
The most refreshing baths.

40/-

I Growl !

This little bear looks rather fierce,
But he's gentle as can be.
Just hear his gentle little growl,
"Oh, won't you please love me ?"

6/11 and 8/11

I Walk so Nicely !

There never was a dog like me.
I've great big feet as you can see,
And my long legs will really walk.
The only thing—I cannot talk.

10/6, 15/6 and 22/6

HARRODS LTD   *Telephone SLOane 1234*   LONDON SW1

Design for the Harrods news of Christmas 1957 by Rowland Enett.
Courtesy Company Archive Harrods Limited

12
WENMEN J. BASSETT-LOWKE

Tom Lowke of J.T.Lowke & Co Ltd was a boilermaker and, after his death his widow married Absalom Bassett. Bassett adopted Tom's son who was called Joseph Tom. When Joseph Tom eventually married and had three sons he added the name Bassett to their names as a gesture to his step father. It was in this way that the surname Bassett-Lowke was created.

One of the three sons, Wenmen Joseph Bassett-Lowke, who was born in 1877, left the family business to found a model engineering company with Harold Franklin in Northampton in 1899. At the same time he also established a working relationship with George Winteringham of Winteringham Ltd who manufactured products for Wenmen's new company.

In 1900 Bassett-Lowke persuaded the three great German toy makers, Bing, Carette and Marklin to produce models specifically for his London store and so a number of British outline locomotives began to appear to the delight of young British enthusiasts. "Bing for Basset-Lowke" was the most common of these and from the beginning of the century live steam 4-4-0 tender locomotives were amongst those models most highly prized by Edwardian youngsters, both in the livery of the London and North Western Railway and called "Black Prince" or "King Edward," and in that of the London and South Western Railway livery.

After the First World War Bing and Marklin continued to manufacture models for Bassett-Lowke but few of their customers were aware that they were made in Germany. At the same time an increasing number of models were manufactured by Bassett-Lowke themselves in Northampton and, in addition to trains and model railways, the company also marketed a limited number of cars and ships which are even rarer today. The model railway range included locomotives of ever increasing accuracy of scale and line from the Great Western Railway, the London Brighton & South Coast Railway, the Caledonian Railway and many others of the period prior to grouping of companies in 1923. After this the London Midland and Scottish Railway, the Southern Railway, the London and North Eastern Railway and the Great Western were all represented in Bassett-Lowke's range. In the years before the Second World War 0 gauge gained in popularity over the larger gauges, partly because model railway enthusiasts wanted to build ever more complex railway layouts and partly because of the tendency for people to live in smaller homes.

One of the most popular 0 gauge models because of its modest price was a 4-4-0 tender loco, which began life as the "Duke of York," went on after the War to become the "Princess Elizabeth" and finally in BR black or blue the "Prince Charles."

Even more popular, for the same reason, was a simple 0-4-0 tank loco with the number 112 on its sides. It was the number of Bassett-Lowke's shop in High Holborn. Customers may have been surprised that on the front of London store were the words "Model Railways. Ships. Architecture." This was because W.J. Bassett-Lowke was a founder member of the Design and Industries Association and another of his interests happened to be the design of houses.

Bassett-Lowke suffered after the Second World War because of the rising tide of 00 gauge model railways which, with Hornby Dublo, had become the natural progression from 0 gauge.

Wenman Bassett-Lowke died in 1953 and all production ceased twelve years later. However the name was not lost as it was revived by Steam Age which offered fine scale models in very limited numbers. Allen Levy of Bassett-Lowke and Steam Age reprinted many of the early Bassett-Lowke catalogues, together with photographs of the highly desirable products for which he himself was responsible and the catalogues both informed and whetted the appetites of many would be collectors.

Bassett-Lowke was taken over by Corgi in 1996 and this resulted in a revival of its fortunes. Amongst other 0 gauge models released by Bassett-Lowke under the ownership of Corgi and made in China was the "Flying Scotsman" in both LNER, with one or two tenders, and British Railways liveries, the Pacific locomotive "Princess Helena Victoria" and the 4-6-0 locomotive "Black Watch." In addition there was the LNER "Humourist" which having been mistakenly finished in Southern Railway colours was soon withdrawn and must now be very rare.

Most recently Corgi was itself taken over by Hornby Hobbies and I watch to see what may result from this development. I for one would love to see a Bassett-Lowke for Hornby Hobbies Great Western Railway Castle in 0 gauge.

An 0 gauge Midland Single

During what now seems to have been a quite brief period in my life, I collected a large number of notable products by Bassett-Lowke, having begun by writing to Bassett-Lowke in London to ask what models they had to offer. I still have the reply I received from Ivan R. Scott in June 1972 in which he listed a Flying Scotsman in BR blue for £65, another in LNER green at £60, a Royal Scot at £55, and a Hornby Princess Elizabeth (boxed) at £125. I bought the LNER "Flying Scotsman" and was pleased to find it to be in good original condition and I also bought from Ivan Scott, a much rarer hand enamelled Bing for Bassett-Lowke 0 gauge Midland Single which had been expertly restored. Originally made in 1920 with the number 650 on its tender sides, the Midland loco's tender had M R applied in two panels. It was a well proportioned model and reflected the period at the end of the nineteenth century when locomotives with just two very larger driving wheels were popular. Whatever might have been their merit there is no doubt that Singles were extremely elegant. In the 1902 Bassett-Lowke catalogue the model was priced at two guineas. Bassett-Lowke wrote of the model that "owing to the increasing weight and speed of modern express trains, locomotives with single driving wheels are now somewhat outclassed, and most lines which previously employed them, including the Great Northern, the home of the famous Stirling "8 footers," and the Great Western, which also had a very large number, have of recent years sent them all to the scrap heap. The Midland, however, still retains over ninety of the handsome and graceful 4-2-2 engines of Mr. S. W. Johnson's design, on which our model of No. 650 is based. These engines are entrusted with various duties, including the haulage of slow and semi-fast passenger trains, but their principle work, at which they excel, is that of piloting both passenger and goods trains – a practice which is in very extensive vogue on the Midland Railway."

0 gauge Midland 'single' and LNWR Black Prince for Bassett-Lowke.

A gauge I Bassett-Lowke Railway

Through an advertisement in the Daily Telegraph I was once offered a gauge I Bassett-Lowke collection of quite breath taking proportions. Every item had been made by Bing or Carette for Bassett-Lowke, and there were three very fine electrically powered models, consisting of an LNWR "King George V," an LNWR 4-4-2 Precursor tank loco, and a Midland 4-4-0. After these were shown on an early evening television programme one viewer kindly offered to exchange a Bassett-Lowke catalogue he had for the Midland loco and tender! In addition there was a colossal number of tinplate LNWR, MR and GWR coaches with opening doors and detailed interiors and, of course, many wagons. One of the coaches was a long and most impressive twelve wheeled Midland Railway dining car with a fitted out interior. The rails alone caused my elderly Triumph 2000 to sit down very low on the road and I drove back to Southampton with extreme care. Back at home I laid all the locomotives and rolling stock out on the lawn and they covered a huge area. It was fortunate that the rectory had extensive lawns.

Hand-enamelled gauge I
LNWR 'George V' and
carriage.

Bing for Bassett-Lowke LNWR
precursor tank loco.

Gauge I Midland 4-4-0 Bing
for Bassett-Lowke.

Coach in early Great Western
livery gauge I.

Gauge I Clerestory Great
Western Railway coach.

A gauge IV "King Edward"

I would recommend anyone who wanted to start a collection of antique toys and model railway items to begin by acquiring if possible the original catalogues or more recent reprints of them. They are invaluable in enabling the collector to know what to look for and how to identify them when they are seen. The 1902 Bassett-Lowke catalogue featured a gauge IV LNWR live steam 4-4-0 monster of a "King Edward" and it was certainly one for me to bear in mind in my quest for early models. In fact I bought my gauge IV "King Edward" from another collector. It was in pieces, although all its parts were there, and it was devoid of its original paint. In contrast the paint on its six wheel tender was crazed with age but otherwise undamaged. It was a project for Chris Littledale, the foremost of all the restorers, and as a result of his expert care, it emerged looking every bit as good as it must have done in 1902. Chris had done no more than to spray a coat of clear varnish over the tender to make its finish match that of the engine and, in its three inch gauge scale, it looked really imposing. I had become accustomed to seeing steam locomotives in dirty BR black during the years before steam was removed from the main line, and it reminded me of how splendid this livery must have looked on the old London and North Western Railway,

Gauge IV 'King Edward' by Bing for Bassett-Lowke.

The LSWR Adams 4-4-0

At that time I was writing a series of monthly articles for the magazine "Automodeller" on early tinplate model cars, boats and trains and, in one edition, I included a photograph of my restored Bing for Bassett-Lowke gauge IV "King Edward." I happened to mention in my article that I would love to have the opportunity to acquire the London and South Western Railway version of the model and unbelievably, not very long afterwards, someone came to my door carrying a large cardboard box in his arms which contained the very model I had mentioned! Its funnel was missing and Bing had mistakenly finished it in Great Northern Railway green instead of that of the London & South Western Railway but it was otherwise in excellent original condition. I was of course delighted to buy it from my caller, in spite of the wisdom in normal circumstances of never buying anything at the door, and I eventually managed to acquire two gauge IV LSWR coaches to go with it. I had a funnel made which was identical to the one that was missing but decided to leave the boiler unpainted because more often than not the boiler paint had become burned off these early models through normal usage.

Gauge IV LSWR Adams 4-4-0.

Gauge I 0-6-2 GNR
Condensing tank loco and
tender.

A gauge I condensing tank loco

I had been to the dentist one afternoon to have a troublesome wisdom tooth extracted and, after the dentist had worked up a sweat trying to pull at it from every conceivable angle with all his might, I felt as though my upper and lower jaws had parted company from each other. But I had arranged to go to an address in Bournemouth early that evening to buy a Bassett-Lowke train so I drove through the New Forest in spite of the intense pain. What I discovered at an address near the sea was a clockwork gauge I Great Northern Railway 0-6-2 Condensing tank loco in extraordinarily good condition. It had certainly been worth my journey and it made me forget all about my pain! It was so absolutely perfect that everyone who saw it afterwards found it hard to believe that it hadn't been expertly restored. Whoever owns it now may indeed have doubts himself but, having met the original owner, I can vouch for it being authentic. Perhaps it stands proudly on the present owner's mantle shelf, his understanding wife allowing it to grace the finest room in her house in a place of honour.

Gauge III clockwork Midland
Railway 0-4-0.

A gauge III Midland 0-4-0

I have always thought that red would be my colour of choice for trains. Not bright red, like Harry Potter's "Hogwarts Express", but deep Midland Railway red, and when I came across a dilapidated gauge III 0-4-0 Midland Railway engine and a four wheel tender, my heart ruled my head and l paid far more to its surprised owner than it was really worth! Its clockwork motor was broken and its paint was in appalling condition, having reached the point when only a complete repaint could redeem it. I surrendered it to the tender mercies of Chris Littledale and, when in due course I received it back, its motor was working again and its glorious livery been fully restored, I was reminded why I had been so enthusiastic about its potential in the first place. I'm glad that I still have a photograph of the gauge III Bing for Bassett-Lowke train loco in its beautifully restored condition.

Gauge III King Edward by Bing
for Bassett-Lowke.

A gauge III LNWR 0-4-0

My LNWR version of the above gauge III engine was unusual in that its extended frame suggested that it was designed for at the very least a 2-4-0 wheel arrangement. However this was not the case and it was merely that Bing and Bassett-Lowke had decided to make their four wheeled model look more impressive. Of course the colours of the old LNWR disappeared when it became absorbed into the LMS but reappeared with British Railways, too often masked by soot and grime.

Live steam gauge I North
London tank loco No 88 from
1902/1903 catalogue.

Great Central Railway 'Sir Sam Fay' with a Caledonian railway Dunalistair.

Gauge I live steam North London tank loco
A tinplate model house boat

I had often admired a model house boat which, being made by Bing for Bassett-Lowke, was featured in the Bassett-Lowke catalogue of 1904/1905. The tinplate craft was made in three sizes and I had the opportunity to buy one of the smallest ones which, being 13.5 inches long, was by no means insignificant. It was flat bottomed and had not, I assumed, been designed to take to the water. It lacked some of the accessories such as flags, Chinese lanterns and chairs which were shown in the illustration but, apart from that, it was essentially complete with its original paint undamaged. The Bing representation of water on the lower half of the hull was so crude that I thought it had been repainted by a child. Fortunately I only disturbed a very small area of its paint-work before establishing that is was in fact original but, all the same, I was most annoyed with myself for doubting its authenticity.

Gauge I scale figures of passengers and railwaymen.

1915 GWR 'City of Bath' with a GNR 4-4-0 at a Hornby station.

13
CONSTRUCTION SETS

Frank Hornby

FRANK HORNBY was born in Liverpool in 1863 where his father was a provision merchant. When he left school at the age of sixteen he worked for his father as a cashier but after his father died, when Frank was twenty-four, he kept the books for David Elliot who was a meat importer in Liverpool.

Frank was fascinated by the tall cranes and gantries in Liverpool docks and when he had married and become the father of Roland, Douglas, and Patricia, he made models of cranes, bridges and lorries to amuse his children. Like most fathers he probably gained at least as much enjoyment in making the models as they had in playing with them. Then he came across a book written by Samuel Smiles entitled "Self Help" and this encouraged him to develop his model making skills on a commercial basis. Crucially it occurred to him hat he could build a range of quite different models from a small number of interchangeable components, which he made by cutting up copper sheets and fixing them together by inserting nuts and bolts through the holes he drilled in the plates and girders that he made. It came to him that the lines of holes in the half inch wide girders could be used not only for nuts and bolts but also for axles and, to Frank's creative mind, the possibilities were endless.

Frank had never been trained as an engineer but in 1901 he had sufficient confidence in his invention to apply for a patent and to seek for a financial backer. David Elliot initially lent him £5 and, when Frank failed to obtain further help from elsewhere, Elliot offered him a room next to his own office where Frank was able to proceed with his project. Clearly David Elliot's help was crucial to Frank Hornby at this early stage in his career. The two became partners and agreed to call Frank's invention "Mechanics Made Easy." The earliest sets were made up of about fifteen tinplate parts and the product was endorsed by Professor Henry Selby Hele-Shaw, the head of the Engineering Department of Liverpool University. The two arranged for other manufacturers to supply the parts and "Mechanics Made Easy" was launched on the market in 1902.

From this humble beginning Hornby and Elliot went from strength to strength and in the first year sold 1,500 of their construction sets. Four years later, with a larger range of more complex sets, the venture began to make a profit for the first time. After this Frank Hornby found that he could manufacture the parts he required for his sets himself on his own premises and he took sole charge of his company.

Meccano Ltd

Frank Hornby founded Meccano Ltd in 1907 with a new factory in Duke Street Liverpool while, at the same time, his elder son Roland set up Meccano (France) Ltd to manufacture Meccano sets in Paris. Frank was soon found it necessary to move his works into a larger building in West Derby Road. In 1914 he moved yet again to the famous Binns Road address where the Company was to remain for sixty-six years. Meccano was also established in Germany but this branch was taken over for military purposes almost immediately by the German Government until the end of the First World War. Surprisingly Frank was able to continue to manufacture his Meccano sets in England throughout the years of the First World War and by the end of the war he employed 1,200 workers on a site which measured 154,000 square feet. In addition the famous toy maker Marklin manufactured Meccano under licence in Germany after the War.

Meccano sets were originally produced with red plates and green girders but the colours were changed in 1934 to dark blue plates with diagonal gold lines which crossed each other to form a regular diamond shaped pattern, while the girders were coloured gold. When Frank Hornby died his two sons stepped into his shoes to ensure the continuance of the Company. Production of Meccano sets, Hornby trains and Dinky Toys had to be suspended during the Second World War as all the factory's resources were diverted to the War effort, and after the War the colours of Meccano reverted to red and green. Meccano sets continued to be offered in different sizes and with different levels of complexity. An illustration of a travelling crane supported on a huge gantry composed entirely of Meccano girders inspired many young builders pit their skills against its challenge. Only the most gifted and committed of youngsters would have proved to be equal to the task. Frank Hornby deliberately incorporated an error in his instructions to stretch young minds even further! Eventually Lego offered a much easier option and Meccano Ltd, undoubtedly suffering from the absence of the towering influence of Frank Hornby, was taken over by the Lines brothers in 1964. The decision was made to go back to the blue and gold colour scheme which had always been used by the Meccano factory in France, but the glory days of Meccano had passed with its founder. Lines Bros was broken up in 1971 and the Meccano was taken over by Airfix, the brilliant manufacturer of plastic kits, the following year. However Lego was proving to be far more popular with its system of interlocking plastic parts being so much easier to assemble than having to come to grips with a screw driver and a spanner. Moreover Lego could be satisfactorily handled by younger children who were attracted to its bright colours. In 1981 Airfix decided that enough was enough and General Mills assumed control of Meccano in the United Kingdom and France. Today Meccano is seeing a revival in its fortunes.

From the 1956 Meccano magazine.

Meccano cars

In the later half of the 1930s Hornby produced a highly colourful range of tinplate model sports cars in three sizes, all of which being much larger than the die cast Dinky Toys. Two cars were offered in the form of construction sets to be assembled with the standard nuts and bolts, and a third was ready assembled. Unlike the normal Meccano sets, these cars were composed of moulded and appropriately coloured parts, so that they made up into very realistic models of the kind of sports cars that the British Motor Industry was producing at the time. Constructor set I offered a range of smaller cars and Constructor set II contained larger models. The car in Constructor set III was already assembled and, in addition to this, there was a range of sports cars of similar character which came complete and were not designed to be taken apart.

Hornby speed boats

Hornby speed boats came fully assembled with no nuts and bolts which might have allowed the ingress of water but they were made of tinplate by the same manufacturer in the 1930s and so are naturally associated with Meccano cars. They all had white decks on red, blue or green hulls. They came in three sizes which ranged from 21.5 cm to 32 cm in length and had such names as Racer I, Racer II, and Racer III, Hawk, Swift, Venture and Viking emblazoned in gold on their hulls. All were beautifully turned out and each was equipped with a strong clockwork motor.

Tri-ang's FIT-BITS SETS

It would have been surprising if Tri-ang had failed to turn its attention to construction sets in the wake of Meccano and they came up with brightly coloured wooden Fit-Bits Sets. Never doing anything by halves, they produced a range which cost from 1/11 to 25 shillings. They have more in common with Lego than Meccano, having patented rubber connections as opposed to nuts and bolts and they were aimed at very young children. As their advertisement indicated, they contained no metal parts and had no sharp edges so that they were ideal for the children for whom they were designed

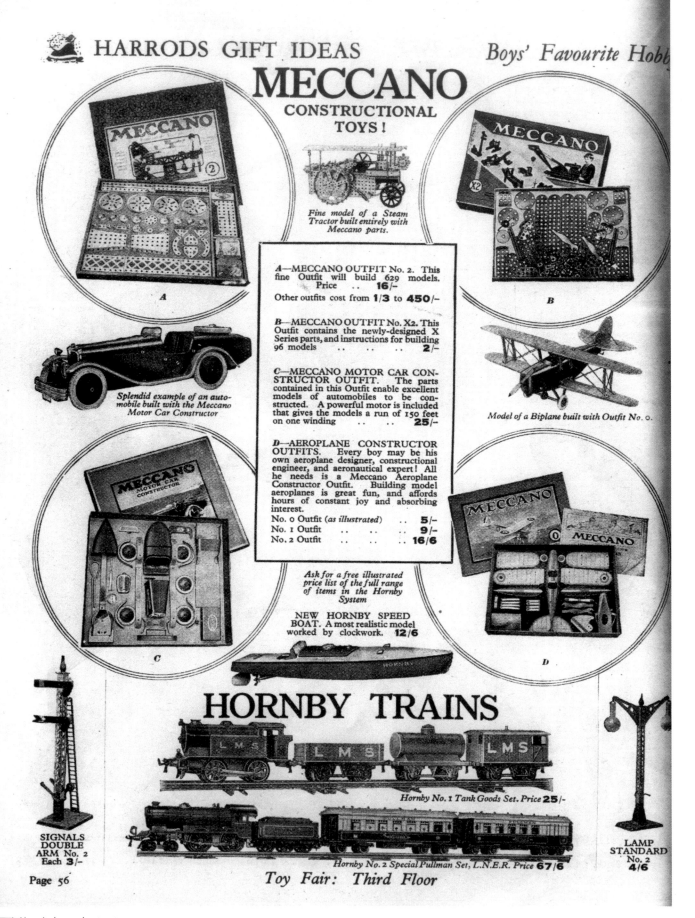

HARRODS GIFT IDEAS

Boys' Favourite Hobb

MECCANO
CONSTRUCTIONAL TOYS!

Fine model of a Steam Tractor built entirely with Meccano parts.

Splendid example of an automobile built with the Meccano Motor Car Constructor

Model of a Biplane built with Outfit No. 0.

A—MECCANO OUTFIT No. 2. This fine Outfit will build 629 models. Price .. **16/-**
Other outfits cost from **1/3** to **450/-**

B—MECCANO OUTFIT No. X2. This Outfit contains the newly-designed X Series parts, and instructions for building 96 models **2/-**

C—MECCANO MOTOR CAR CONSTRUCTOR OUTFIT. The parts contained in this Outfit enable excellent models of automobiles to be constructed. A powerful motor is included that gives the models a run of 150 feet on one winding **25/-**

D—AEROPLANE CONSTRUCTOR OUTFITS. Every boy may be his own aeroplane designer, constructional engineer, and aeronautical expert! All he needs is a Meccano Aeroplane Constructor Outfit. Building model aeroplanes is great fun, and affords hours of constant joy and absorbing interest.
No. 0 Outfit (*as illustrated*) .. **5/-**
No. 1 Outfit **9/-**
No. 2 Outfit **16/6**

Ask for a free illustrated price list of the full range of items in the Hornby System

NEW HORNBY SPEED BOAT. A most realistic model worked by clockwork. **12/6**

HORNBY TRAINS

Hornby No. 1 Tank Goods Set. Price **25/-**

SIGNALS DOUBLE ARM No. 2 Each **3/-**

LAMP STANDARD No. 2 **4/6**

Hornby No. 2 Special Pullman Set, L.N.E.R. Price **67/6**

Toy Fair: Third Floor

Page 56

Frank Hornby's products at the Harrods toy fair in 1932.

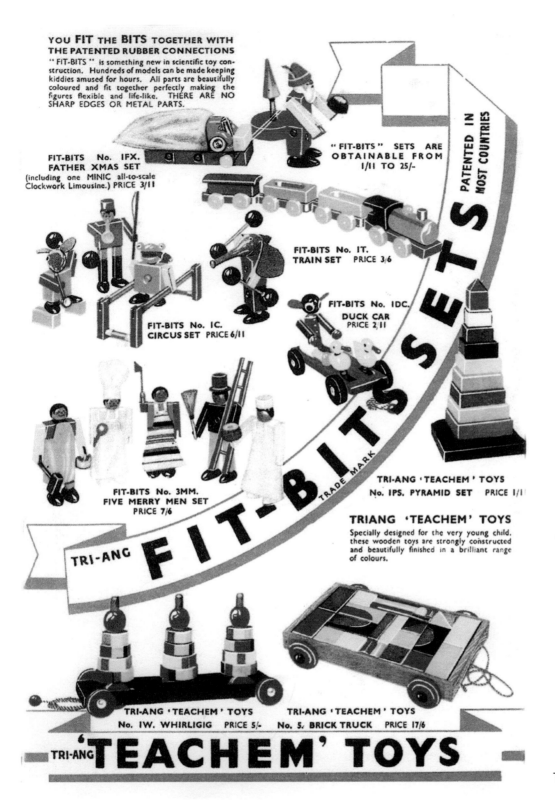

Tri-ang's construction toys.

Minic Construction sets

Tri-ang also produced Minic Construction sets in the 1930s based upon their extensive range of clockwork tinplate vehicles. They were fairly undemanding but must have been extremely popular with those lucky enough to receive them as birthday or Christmas presents. The No 1 set had enough parts to assemble six types of vehicles and included brushes and enamel paints. Just the thing for the long dark winter evenings!

Lego

Ole Kirk Christiansen first made wooden toys in 1932 in Billund in Denmark. Two years later he named his products Lego from the Danish words meaning "Play well." In Latin the brand name can also mean even more appropriately "I put together."

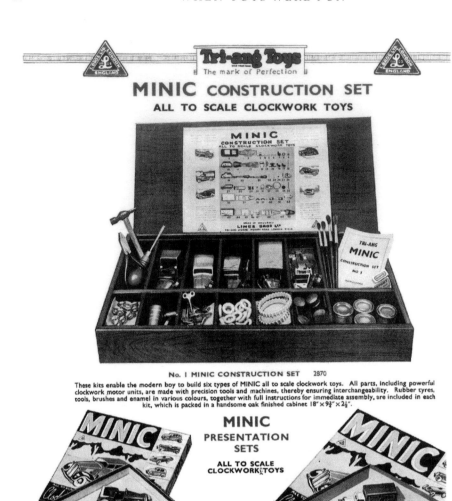

Minic construction set.

A fire destroyed the Lego factory in 1942 but it was rebuilt and in 1947 the important step was taken to make plastic injection toys.

The first products were called Automatic Binding Bricks and they were not called Lego bricks until 1951. An immensely popular range of building sets was marketed in the years that followed and the system by which the bricks were joined together was patented. After the death of Ole his son Godtfred Kirk Christiansen succeeded him and eventually his son, Kjeld Kirk Christiansen, took his place. In 1963 cellulous acetate was replaced by acrylonitrite butadiene stryrene which improved the colour and the durability of Lego bricks, and Lego sets were made which built up a range of cars and other vehicles. Duplo entered the field in 1967, this being a larger brick for smaller children and, with the influence of TV and films, figures from Star Wars and the Ninja Turtles were added to the range.

The success of Lego world wide has been phenomenal, the colourful and easy to assemble bricks seeming to be much less daunting than the earlier Meccano system with its nuts and bolts. At the same time Techno Lego tested the most technically advanced young builders to the full.

Airfix

Airfix, like Revell, has been a popular manufacturer of construction kits with older children for many years, and it all began by accident. Originally founded by a Hungarian refugee called Nicholas Kove in 1939, Airfix produced rubber toys which were, as the name suggests, inflated with air. After the War Nicholas made plastic combs and, in so doing, adopted the process of injection moulding. This led Harry Ferguson to invite him to produce models of his tractor in plastic as a sales tool. This posed a problem which was solved by the manufacture of a number of separate parts which were then assembled by his employees. The tractors were also sold as toys using the Airfix brand name, and it soon became apparent that they could be marketed more cheaply sold as kits for the purchaser to assemble. The models also proved to be even more popular in this form and in 1952 a model of the Golden Hinde appeared on the shelves of Woolworth's stores. The next year it was joined by a Spitfire and, as anyone who was around at the time will know, the range grew and grew. Airfix kits of various scales and degrees of complexity were made of ships, cars, motorcycles, and both commercial and military vehicles.

In the 1980s Airfix fell on hard times, partly because of the rising price of oil, and therefore of plastic, and partly because of increasing competition from computer games. In consequence Airfix was taken over by General Mills which in turn was taken over by the Borden of the Hobby Products Group. In 1995 Borden sold Airfix, together with Humbrol, to an Irish company and in 2006 it passed to Hornby Hobbies Ltd. Airfix flourishes again with over a hundred new kits being introduced in the current year.

14
HORNBY TRAINS

FRANK HORNBY first began to produce 0 gauge Hornby trains in 1927 and they were constructed with tin plate parts bolted together on the same principle as Meccano. They were powered in the early years by clockwork motors manufactured by Marklin in Germany. Most of the trains and rolling stock were made to vaguely resemble British railway companies and immediately acquired a large and growing number of loyal and enthusiastic followers. Hornby trains were well made and built to last.

Cover of 1925 *The Hornby Book of Trains* .

The very first Hornby train, which was Frank's prototype, looked as if unpainted pieces of Meccano had been bolted together in the general shape of a railway engine, and the earliest Hornby trains which were produced commercially, being fastened together by the same means, were intended to be taken to pieces and rebuilt as well as being run on rails. The greatest number of Hornby train sets consisted of four wheeled locos with four wheeled tenders accompanied by either two carriages or one wagon, each also with four wheels, and they were finished in pre 1923 liveries such as that of the Great Northern Railway and the Midland Railway. After 1923 they were available in the liveries of the four British railway companies. Hornby also produced sets of four wheeled tank locos with three wagons which began with the least expensive M0 sets and progressed through the M1 and M2 sets to the No. 1 and No 1 Special sets. The more desirable No. 2 4-4-4 tank locos were also made in the four British liveries and in recent years these been reproduced by Ace Trains.

At the top end of the range there was a series of 4-4-0 locomotives with six wheel tenders the earliest of which were of a simple generic design while the later range faithfully reflected the lines of actual trains. The "Scarborough Flier" was a good repre-

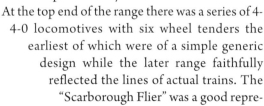

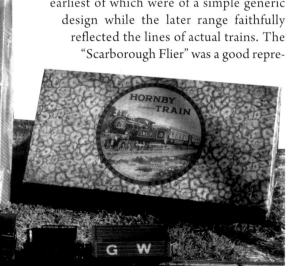

1920s Hornby train set and two hornby boxes.

Top left: Two early Hornby trains alongside a Hornby station *Top right:* Hornby LMS compound with Pullman coach.

sentation of the LNER "Brabham Moor", the "Folkestone Flyer" an accurate model of a Southern Railway "L.1" Class locomotive, "The Yorkshireman" was an LMS "Standard Compound" and "The Bristolian" a Great Western Railway "County of Bedford." In addition there was a Schools Class "Eton." Then there was a range of 4-4-2 locomotives with six wheeled tenders, identical under the paintwork, and nominally representing the LMS "Royal Scott", the LNER "Flying Scotsman", the Great Western "Cornish Riviera Express" and the Southern Railway "Golden Arrow". A fifth train in the series was the French Riviera "Blue" train set with a brown Nord locomotive and both dining and sleeping cars in the appropriate livery. The Hornby Metropolitan train set naturally had a quite distinctive outline.

'Bramham Moor' and two Hornby pullman coaches.

In the 1930s the No 2 Special 4-4-4 tank locomotives were replaced by restyled 4-4-2 tank locomotives in the four liveries. There was the option of clockwork or electric power throughout the range. Railway stations, foot bridges, level crossings, tunnels and signals were also available with quantities of rails. The nuts and bolts disappeared in the course of the 1920s and instead the plates were fastened together more conventionally by metal flanges.

The most expensive model of all in the 1930s Hornby range was the LMS Pacific locomotive "Princess Elizabeth", introduced just before the Second World War. Pulling a rake of LMS coaches or the Pullman "Iolanthe" and "Marjorie", it was a worthy rival to its Bassett-Lowke counterpart.

Frank Hornby, who had became a Member of Parliament in 1931, died in 1938.

After the Second World War, during which time all production of model railways had ceased, the Hornby 0 gauge range was confined to 0-4-0 tank and tender locomotives and four wheel coaches and wagons.

The inexpensive M0 engine and tender became known as No. 20 and the pre-war M1 appeared again either in red or green, with the number 3435 on the tender sides, representing the date when it appeared in its later form. In 1956 a new No 30 engine appeared with the number 45746 on the sides of its cab. Next up after the War was the M3 tank loco now called the 101 and available with black British Railways livery, LMS red numbered 2270 and LNER green numbered 460. They were more expensive and robust with coupled wheels and a reversing mechanism. Finally the pre-war No 1 tender engine re-emerged after the War with a more powerful motor than the 101 tank models and it was available in BR black or green, and in LMS and LNER. liveries.

Post-war Hornby collection.

0 gauge Hornby locos had become far less popular than Hornby Dublo and the last to be withdrawn was the M0 in 1968.

Collecting Hornby trains

As a collector in the 1970s I discovered that a considerable quantity of Pre-War Hornby train sets had survived, most of which had been gathering dust for many years, and it wasn't too difficult or costly to assemble a very comprehensive collection. Like most others, I found it impossible to build a permanent layout of 0 gauge scale but occasionally put together a track to enable trains to circulate around my study before turning into the hall and from there into the lounge where they would negotiate a large circle right around the room before returning to the study. With two parallel tracks and two trains made up of, for example, 4-4-2 tank engines each pulling four or five eight wheeled coaches, one in LMS colours and the other in those of the LNER, they made a fine show. A few years ago I saw a very impressive 0 gauge layout by Ace Trains at Fortnum and Masons of repro Hornby trains which reminded me of my Hornby collection was by then long gone.

Hornby Dublo

Hornby Dublo was introduced in 1938 some time after Bing had marketed their Table Top Railway in this smaller gauge with tinplate locomotives, wagons and coaches. 00 gauge clearly offered the important advantage of being able to accomplish much more within a given space. At this time the average young train operators were living in houses which were much smaller than those who, prior to 1914 fired up their gauge IV live steam models in their ample lofts, so the future looked set fair for the new Hornby Dublo. Their locomotives were produced with substantial diecast bodies and their wagons and coaches were made of tinplate. The range included a 2-6-4 tank loco, a 4-6-2 Duchess Class loco, a 4-6-2 A4, a 4-6-0 Castle and a 2-4-0 freight locomotive. The last two had die cast tenders while the others were of tinplate like the coaches. In addition three green British Railways Diesel-Electric locomotives were added to the range after the War, an 0-6-0 shunting locomotive, a Bo-Bo locomotive with eight wheels, and a Co-Bo model with its ten wheels.

Frank Hornby's eldest son Roland sold the business in 1964 to Lines Brothers and therefore to Tri-ang Railways.

Wrenn took over Hornby Dublo and, for a time the range appeared in the Tri-ang Hornby catalogue.

A collection of 00 gauge Tri-ang Hornby, Hornby and Wrenn locos and coaches.

MO Passenger Set. This set contains Locomotive (non-reversible), Tender, one Pullman Coach and set of Rails. One of the rails is a Brake Rail, by means of which the train may be braked from the track. The set is richly coloured and well finished. Gauge 0 .. .. **Price 6/-**

M1 Passenger Set. (As illustrated.) This set is similar to the MO Passenger Set, excepting that it has two Pullman Coaches instead of one, and additional Rails .. **7/6**

M2 Passenger Set. This set is also similar to the MO Passenger Set, but it has three Pullman Coaches instead of one, and additional Rails **9/-**

The components of the M Passenger Sets may be purchased separately, if required. The prices are as follows :—

M Locomotive (without Tender) .. .. **Price 3/-**   **M Tender** .. .. .. **Price 9d.**   **M Pullman Coach** .. **Price 1/-**

M Goods Set. This strongly-built train set contains Locomotive, Tender, two M Wagons (L.M.S.R., L.N.E.R., G.W.R. or S.R.) and set of Rails. A rail fitted with a special braking device is included. The Locomotive, which is non-reversible, is fitted with an efficient brake mechanism. Gauge 0 .. .. **Price 8/6**

The components of the M Goods Set may be purchased separately, if required. The prices are as follows :—

M Locomotive (without Tender) .. .. **Price 3/-**   **M Tender** .. .. **Price 9d.**   **M Wagon** .. .. **Price 1/3**

The separate prices of Hornby Rails, Points and Crossings are specified on page 34.

Page Twelve

From a 1920s Hornby catalogue

HORNBY No. 0 GOODS SET, L.N.E.R.

This set contains Loco, Tender, one Wagon, and Rails as in the No. 0 Goods L.M.S., and is identical with that set except for the lettering. It is supplied with either green or black loco and tender and the colour required should be stated when ordering. Richly enamelled in realistic colours and highly finished. Gauge 0.

Hornby No. 0 Goods Set, L.N.E.R., complete, packed in strong cardboard box, Price 17/6

HORNBY No. 0 PASSENGER SET, L.N.E.R.

The contents of this set are similar to those of the No. 0 Passenger L.M.S., namely, Loco, Tender, two Coaches, and Rails to form a circle of 2-ft. diameter and two Straight Rails (including one brake rail). The Loco is fitted with brake mechanism. Non-reversible type. Gauge 0.

Hornby No. 0 Passenger Set, L.N.E.R., complete, packed in strong cardboard box, Price 22/6

HORNBY No. 0 GOODS AND PASSENGER SETS, G.W.

The No. 0 Goods and Passenger Sets are also lettered to represent G.W. rolling stock. In each case the locos and tenders are coloured Great Western green only. The contents of each set are similar to those in the L.M.S. and L.N.E.R. sets.

Hornby No. 0 Goods Set, G.W., complete, packed in strong cardboard box, Price 17/6   Hornby No. 0 Passenger Set, G.W., complete, packed in strong cardboard box, Price 22/6

The Locos, Tenders, Coaches and Wagons of the above train sets may also be purchased separately. Prices are as follows :—

Hornby No. 0 Loco ... ... Price 10/6		Hornby Passenger Coach ... ... Price 3/6
Hornby Tender ... ... ,, 2/6		Hornby Wagon ... ... ,, 2/6

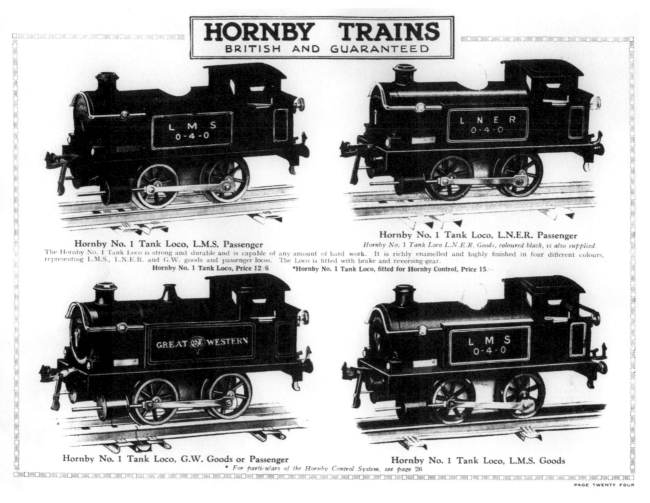

HORNBY TRAINS
BRITISH AND GUARANTEED

Hornby No. 1 Tank Loco, L.M.S. Passenger

Hornby No. 1 Tank Loco, L.N.E.R. Passenger
Hornby No. 1 Tank Loco L.N.E.R. Goods, coloured black, is also supplied.

The Hornby No. 1 Tank Loco is strong and durable and is capable of any amount of hard work. It is richly enamelled and highly finished in four different colours, representing L.M.S., L.N.E.R. and G.W. goods and passenger locos. The Loco is fitted with brake and reversing-gear.

Hornby No. 1 Tank Loco, Price 12/6   *****Hornby No. 1 Tank Loco, fitted for Hornby Control, Price 15/—**

Hornby No. 1 Tank Loco, G.W. Goods or Passenger

Hornby No. 1 Tank Loco, L.M.S. Goods

* For particulars of the Hornby Control System, see page 26

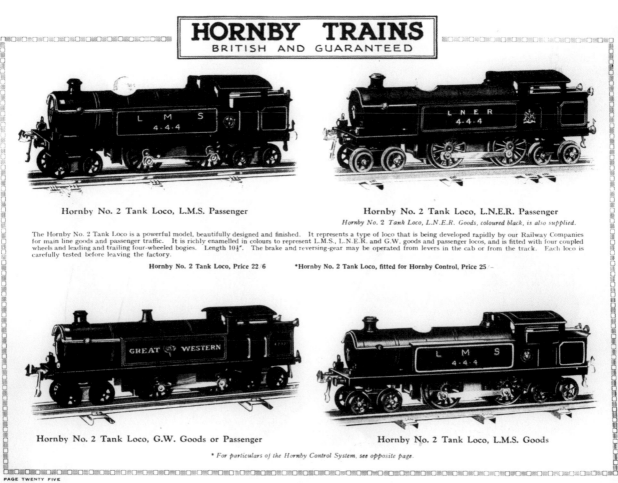

HORNBY TRAINS
BRITISH AND GUARANTEED

Hornby No. 2 Tank Loco, L.M.S. Passenger

Hornby No. 2 Tank Loco, L.N.E.R. Passenger
Hornby No. 2 Tank Loco, L.N.E.R. Goods, coloured black, is also supplied.

The Hornby No. 2 Tank Loco is a powerful model, beautifully designed and finished. It represents a type of loco that is being developed rapidly by our Railway Companies for main line goods and passenger traffic. It is richly enamelled in colours to represent L.M.S., L.N.E.R. and G.W. goods and passenger locos, and is fitted with four coupled wheels and leading and trailing four-wheeled bogies. Length 10¾". The brake and reversing-gear may be operated from levers in the cab or from the track. Each loco is carefully tested before leaving the factory.

Hornby No. 2 Tank Loco, Price 22/6   *****Hornby No. 2 Tank Loco, fitted for Hornby Control, Price 25/—**

Hornby No. 2 Tank Loco, G.W. Goods or Passenger

Hornby No. 2 Tank Loco, L.M.S. Goods

* For particulars of the Hornby Control System, see opposite page.

HORNBY TRAINS
BRITISH AND GUARANTEED

HORNBY No. 2 TANK PASSENGER SET, L.N.E.R.

This set contains a Hornby No. 2 Tank Loco, three Passenger Coaches, Guard's Van and Rails as in the No. 2 Tank Passenger Set L.M.S., described on the opposite page but the lettering and colouring are representative of L.N.E.R. Locos and rolling stock.   Gauge 0.

Hornby No. 2 Tank Passenger Set, L.N.E.R., complete, well boxed, Price 40/-

*Hornby No. 2 Tank Passenger Set, L.N.E.R., complete, well boxed, fitted for Hornby Control, Price 45/-

HORNBY No. 2 TANK PASSENGER SET, G.W.

The contents of this set are identical with those of the L.M.S. and L.N.E.R. sets, except that they are coloured and lettered to represent G.W. rolling stock.

Hornby No. 2 Tank Passenger Set, G.W., complete, well boxed, Price 40/-

*Hornby No. 2 Tank Passenger Set, G.W., complete, well boxed, fitted for Hornby Control, Price 45/-

HORNBY No. 2 TANK GOODS SET, L.N.E.R.

No. 2 Tank Goods Set L.N.E.R. consists of a No. 2 Tank Loco, Hornby Wagon, Petrol Tank Wagon, No. 1 Cattle Truck, Brake Van and set of Rails including one brake rail. It is supplied with either green or black loco and the colour required should be stated when ordering.   Gauge 0.

Hornby No. 2 Tank Goods Set, L.N.E.R., complete, well boxed, Price 37/6

*Hornby No. 2 Tank Goods Set, L.N.E.R., complete, well boxed, fitted for Hornby Control, Price 42/6

HORNBY No. 2 TANK GOODS SET, G.W.

No. 2 Tank Goods Set is also available with G.W. lettering and colouring.   The loco in this set is only supplied in Great Western green.   The contents of the set are exactly the same as those of the L.M.S. and L.N.E.R. sets.

Hornby No. 2 Tank Goods Set, G.W., complete, well boxed, Price 37/6

*Hornby No. 2 Tank Goods Set, G.W., complete, well boxed, fitted for Hornby Control, Price 42/6

The components of the above train sets may also be purchased separately if required.   Prices are as follows :—

Hornby No. 2 Tank Loco	... ... Price 22/6	Petrol Tank Wagon	... ...	Price 2/6
Hornby Passenger Coach	,, 3/6	Brake Van ...	... ...	,, 3/6
Hornby Wagon	,, 2/6	No. 1 Cattle Truck ...	... ...	,, 3/6

*Hornby No. 2 Tank Loco, fitted for Hornby Control, Price 25

* For particulars of the Hornby Control System, see page 26

HORNBY TRAINS
BRITISH AND GUARANTEED

Clockwork

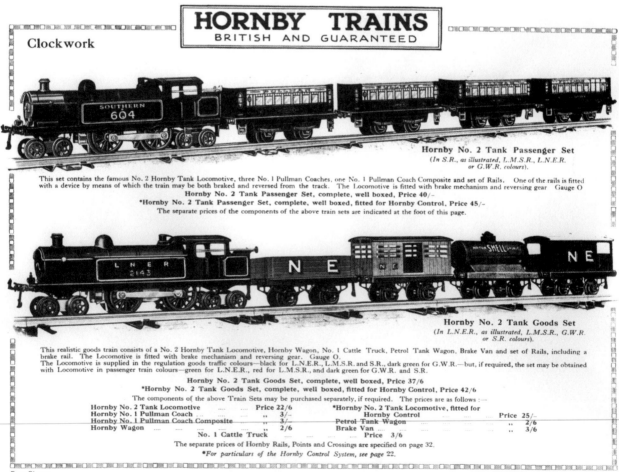

Hornby No. 2 Tank Passenger Set
(In S.R., as illustrated, L.M.S.R., L.N.E.R. or G.W.R. colours).

This set contains the famous No. 2 Hornby Tank Locomotive, three No. 1 Pullman Coaches, one No. 1 Pullman Coach Composite and set of Rails.   One of the rails is fitted with a device by means of which the train may be both braked and reversed from the track.   The Locomotive is fitted with brake mechanism and reversing gear   Gauge O

Hornby No. 2 Tank Passenger Set, complete, well boxed, Price 40/-

*Hornby No. 2 Tank Passenger Set, complete, well boxed, fitted for Hornby Control, Price 45/-

The separate prices of the components of the above train sets are indicated at the foot of this page.

Hornby No. 2 Tank Goods Set
(In L.N.E.R., as illustrated, L.M.S.R., G.W.R. or S.R. colours).

This realistic goods train consists of a No. 2 Hornby Tank Locomotive, Hornby Wagon, No. 1 Cattle Truck, Petrol Tank Wagon, Brake Van and set of Rails, including a brake rail. The Locomotive is fitted with brake mechanism and reversing gear. Gauge O.

The Locomotive is supplied in the regulation goods traffic colours—black for L.N.E.R., L.M.S.R. and S.R., dark green for G.W.R.—but, if required, the set may be obtained with Locomotive in passenger train colours—green for L.N.E.R., red for L.M.S.R., and dark green for G.W.R. and S.R.

Hornby No. 2 Tank Goods Set, complete, well boxed, Price 37/6

*Hornby No. 2 Tank Goods Set, complete, well boxed, fitted for Hornby Control, Price 42/6

The components of the above Train Sets may be purchased separately, if required.   The prices are as follows :—

Hornby No. 2 Tank Locomotive	... Price 22/6	*Hornby No. 2 Tank Locomotive, fitted for	
Hornby No. 1 Pullman Coach ...	,, 3/-	Hornby Control	Price 25/-
Hornby No. 1 Pullman Coach Composite	,, 3/-	Petrol Tank Wagon	,, 2/6
Hornby Wagon ...	,, 2/6	Brake Van	,, 3/6
	No. 1 Cattle Truck	... ... Price 3/6	

The separate prices of Hornby Rails, Points and Crossings are specified on page 32.

*For particulars of the Hornby Control System, see page 22.

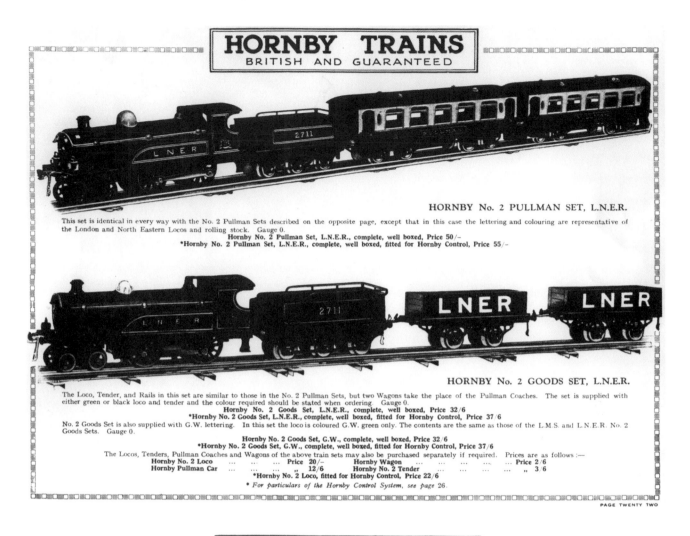

HORNBY TRAINS
BRITISH AND GUARANTEED

HORNBY No. 2 PULLMAN SET, L.N.E.R.

This set is identical in every way with the No. 2 Pullman Sets described on the opposite page, except that in this case the lettering and colouring are representative of the London and North Eastern Locos and rolling stock. Gauge 0.

Hornby No. 2 Pullman Set, L.N.E.R., complete, well boxed, Price 50/-
*Hornby No. 2 Pullman Set, L.N.E.R., complete, well boxed, fitted for Hornby Control, Price 55/-

HORNBY No. 2 GOODS SET, L.N.E.R.

The Loco, Tender, and Rails in this set are similar to those in the No. 2 Pullman Sets, but two Wagons take the place of the Pullman Coaches. The set is supplied with either green or black loco and tender and the colour required should be stated when ordering. Gauge 0.

Hornby No. 2 Goods Set, L.N.E.R., complete, well boxed, Price 32/6
*Hornby No. 2 Goods Set, L.N.E.R., complete, well boxed, fitted for Hornby Control, Price 37/6

No. 2 Goods Set is also supplied with G.W. lettering. In this set the loco is coloured G.W. green only. The contents are the same as those of the L.M.S. and L.N.E.R. No. 2 Goods Sets. Gauge 0.

Hornby No. 2 Goods Set, G.W., complete, well boxed, Price 32/6
*Hornby No. 2 Goods Set, G.W., complete, well boxed, fitted for Hornby Control, Price 37/6

The Locos, Tenders, Pullman Coaches and Wagons of the above train sets may also be purchased separately if required. Prices are as follows :—

Hornby No. 2 Loco ... ... Price 20/-   Hornby Wagon ... ... Price 2/6
Hornby Pullman Car ... ... " 12/6   Hornby No. 2 Tender ... ... " 3/6
*Hornby No. 2 Loco, fitted for Hornby Control, Price 22/6

* For particulars of the Hornby Control System, see page 26.

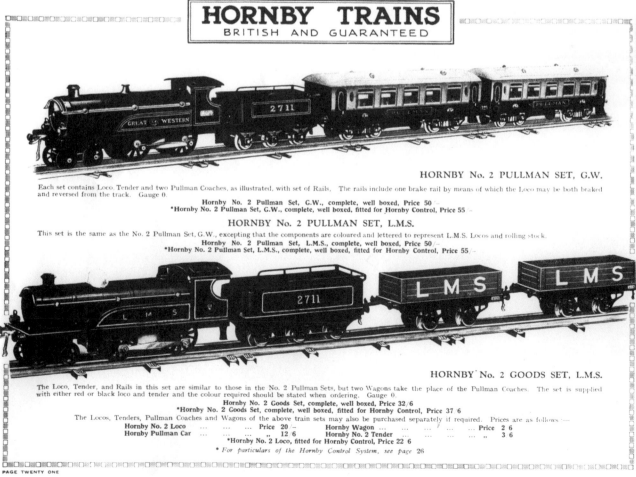

HORNBY TRAINS
BRITISH AND GUARANTEED

HORNBY No. 2 PULLMAN SET, G.W.

Each set contains Loco, Tender and two Pullman Coaches, as illustrated, with set of Rails. The rails include one brake rail by means of which the Loco may be both braked and reversed from the track. Gauge 0.

Hornby No. 2 Pullman Set, G.W., complete, well boxed, Price 50/-
*Hornby No. 2 Pullman Set, G.W., complete, well boxed, fitted for Hornby Control, Price 55/-

HORNBY No. 2 PULLMAN SET, L.M.S.

This set is the same as the No. 2 Pullman Set, G.W., excepting that the components are coloured and lettered to represent L.M.S. Locos and rolling stock.

Hornby No. 2 Pullman Set, L.M.S., complete, well boxed, Price 50/-
*Hornby No. 2 Pullman Set, L.M.S., complete, well boxed, fitted for Hornby Control, Price 55/-

HORNBY No. 2 GOODS SET, L.M.S.

The Loco, Tender, and Rails in this set are similar to those in the No. 2 Pullman Sets, but two Wagons take the place of the Pullman Coaches. The set is supplied with either red or black loco and tender and the colour required should be stated when ordering. Gauge 0.

Hornby No. 2 Goods Set, complete, well boxed, Price 32/6
*Hornby No. 2 Goods Set, complete, well boxed, fitted for Hornby Control, Price 37/6

The Locos, Tenders, Pullman Coaches and Wagons of the above train sets may also be purchased separately if required. Prices are as follows :—

Hornby No. 2 Loco ... ... Price 20/-   Hornby Wagon ... ... Price 2/6
Hornby Pullman Car ... ... " 12/6   Hornby No. 2 Tender ... ... " 3/6
*Hornby No. 2 Loco, fitted for Hornby Control, Price 22/6

* For particulars of the Hornby Control System, see page 26

From a late 1930s Hornby catalogue

Gauge O, 1¼ in.

The Royal Scot

Golden Arrow

The Train Sets listed on this page carry the names of famous British Expresses, as follows:—

"The Royal Scot"
L.M.S.

"The Flying Scotsman"
L.N.E.R.

"Cornish Riviera Express"
G.W.R.

"The Golden Arrow"
S.R.

No. 3C Clockwork Passenger Train Set "The Royal Scot". L.M.S.

No. 3C Clockwork Pullman Train Set "The Golden Arrow". S.R.

The components of the Train Sets shown on this page are obtainable separately at the following prices:—

E320 Electric Locomotive (20-volt) automatic reversing (without Tender) Price	32/6
No. 3C Clockwork Locomotive, reversing (without Tender) Price	22/6
No. 2 Special Tender ... Price	6/-
No. 2 Corridor Coach ... Price	7/6
No. 2 Corridor Composite Coach ... Price	7/6
No. 2 Special Pullman Coach ... Price	13/-
No. 2 Special Pullman Coach Composite Price	13/-

The prices of Hornby Rails are given in pages 49, 50 and 51.
For particulars and prices of Transformers, see page 34.

HORNBY
E320 ELECTRIC and No. 3C CLOCKWORK PASSENGER TRAIN SETS
L.M.S., L.N.E.R. or G.W.R.

20-VOLT ELECTRIC—AUTOMATIC REVERSING

E320 (20-volt). Locomotive (automatic reversing) with electric headlamp, No. 2 Special Tender, two No. 2 Corridor Coaches, one No. 2 Corridor Composite Coach, twelve EA2 Curved Rails, four EB1 Straight Rails and a Terminal Connecting Plate. Space required—6 ft. 3 in. by 4 ft. 6 in. Price **67/6**

CLOCKWORK

No. 3C (Clockwork). Locomotive (reversing), No. 2 Special Tender, one No. 2 Corridor Coach, one No. 2 Corridor Composite Coach, twelve A2 Curved Rails, three B1 Straight Rails and a BBR Straight Brake and Reverse Rail by means of which the Train can be either braked or reversed from the track. Space required—6 ft. 3 in. by 4 ft. 6 in. Price **47/6**

HORNBY E320 ELECTRIC and No. 3C CLOCKWORK PULLMAN TRAIN SETS (S.R. only)

20-VOLT ELECTRIC—AUTOMATIC REVERSING

E320 (20-volt). Locomotive (automatic reversing) with electric headlamp, No. 2 Special Tender, one No. 2 Special Pullman Coach, one No. 2 Special Pullman Coach Composite, twelve EA2 Curved Rails, four EB1 Straight Rails and a Terminal Connecting Plate. Space required—6 ft. 3 in. by 4 ft. 6 in. Price **70/-**

CLOCKWORK

No. 3C (Clockwork). Locomotive (reversing), No. 2 Special Tender, one No. 2 Special Pullman Coach, one No. 2 Special Pullman Coach Composite, twelve A2 Curved Rails, three B1 Straight Rails and one BBR Straight Brake and Reverse Rail by means of which the Train can be either braked or reversed from the track. Space required—6 ft. 3 in. by 4 ft. 6 in. Price **58/6**

If you are interested in Deferred Payment Terms turn to page 49.

HORNBY "TRUE TO TYPE" PASSENGER TRAIN SETS
FAMOUS TRAINS HAULED BY FAMOUS LOCOMOTIVES

Gauge O, 1¼ in.

THE BRISTOLIAN

THE YORKSHIREMAN

No. 2 Special Clockwork Passenger Train Set. G.W.R.

No. 2 Special Clockwork Passenger Train Set. L.M.S.

No. 2 Special Clockwork Passenger Train Set. S.R.

HORNBY
E220 SPECIAL ELECTRIC and No. 2 SPECIAL CLOCKWORK PASSENGER TRAIN SETS

20-VOLT ELECTRIC—AUTOMATIC REVERSING

E220 Special (20-volt). Locomotive (automatic reversing) with electric headlamp, one No. 2 Special Tender, two No. 2 Corridor Coaches, one No. 2 Corridor Composite Coach, twelve EA2 Curved Rails, two EB1 Straight Rails and a Terminal Connecting Plate. Space required—5 ft. 4 in. by 4 ft. 6 in. Price **72/-**

CLOCKWORK

No. 2 Special (Clockwork). Locomotive (reversing), one No. 2 Special Tender, one No. 2 Corridor Coach, one No. 2 Corridor Composite Coach, twelve A2 Curved Rails, one B1 Straight Rail and one BBR Straight Brake and Reverse Rail by means of which the Train can be either braked or reversed from the track. Space required—5 ft. 4 in. by 4 ft. 6 in. Price **52/-**

The components of the above Train Sets can be purchased separately. For prices see foot of opposite page.

"Folkestone Flyer" (S.R.)
hauled by the "L1" Class Locomotive "No. 1759"

"The Scarborough Flier" (L.N.E.R.)
hauled by the "Hunt" Class Locomotive "The Bramham Moor"

"The Bristolian" (G.W.R.)
hauled by the "County" Class Locomotive "County of Bedford"

"The Yorkshireman" (L.M.S.)
hauled by the "Standard Compound" Class Locomotive "No. 1185"

"The Scarborough Flier"

E220 Special Electric Passenger Train Set, L.N.E.R.

"THE SCARBOROUGH FLIER" is a famous L.N.E.R. train that runs between London (King's Cross) and Scarborough, providing a speedy service to the famous Yorkshire coast resort. It is a particularly popular train, and on the first part of the down journey to York it is timed at an average start-to-stop speed of 63 m.p.h. Leaving King's Cross at 11-10 a.m. it brings Scarborough within a four-hour journey from London.

The Hornby 20-volt electric and clockwork models of "The Scarborough Flier" have all the fine characteristics of their prototype. They are available in complete train sets, as detailed on the opposite page, or the components can be purchased separately at the prices indicated at the foot of this page.

"The Bramham Moor" E220 Special Electric Locomotive (20-volt) automatic reversing, with Tender.

If you are interested in Deferred Payment Terms turn to page 49.

The components of the E220 Special Electric and No. 2 Special Clockwork Passenger Train Sets are obtainable separately at the following prices:—

E220 Special Electric Locomotive (20-volt) automatic reversing (without Tender)	Price 37/6
No. 2 Special Clockwork Locomotive, reversing (without Tender)	Price 27/6
No. 2 Special Tender ... Price 6/-	No. 2 Corridor Coach ... Price 7/6
No. 2 Corridor Composite Coach ...	Price 7/6

The prices of Hornby Rails are given in pages 49, 50 and 51. For particulars and prices of Transformers see page 34.

HORNBY *Riviera "Blue"* TRAIN SETS

Gauge O, 1¼ in.

ELECTRIC OR CLOCKWORK

No. 3C Clockwork Riviera "Blue" Passenger Train Set

20-VOLT ELECTRIC—AUTOMATIC REVERSING

E320 (20-volt). Locomotive (automatic reversing) with electric headlamp, No. 3 Riviera "Blue" Tender, Riviera "Blue" Dining Car, Riviera "Blue" Sleeping Car, twelve EA2 Curved Rails, four EB1 Straight Rails and a Terminal Connecting Plate. Space required—6 ft. 3 in. by 4 ft. 6 in. The Set is supplied in correct Riviera "Blue" Train Colours   Price 65/-

CLOCKWORK

No. 3c (Clockwork). Locomotive (reversing), No. 3 Riviera "Blue" Tender, Riviera "Blue" Dining Car, Riviera "Blue" Sleeping Car, twelve A2 Curved Rails, three B1 Straight Rails and a BBR1 Straight Brake and Reverse Rail by means of which the Train can be either braked or reversed from the track. Space required—6 ft. 3 in. by 4 ft. 6 in. The Set is supplied in correct Riviera "Blue" Train colours.   Price 52/0

The components of the Riviera "Blue" Train Sets are obtainable separately at the following prices:—

E320 Electric Riviera "Blue" Locomotive (20-volt) automatic reversing.	Price 32/6
No. 3C Clockwork Riviera "Blue" Locomotive, reversing.	Price 22/6
No. 3 Riviera "Blue" Tender.	Price 4/6
Riviera "Blue" Dining Car or Sleeping Car.	Price, each, 10/6

The prices of Hornby Rails, Points and Crossings are given in pages 49, 50 and 51. For particulars and prices of Transformers see page 34.

If you are interested in Deferred Payment Terms turn to page 49

Hornby No. 3C Clockwork Metropolitan Train Set

6-VOLT ELECTRIC

E36 (6-volt). Locomotive (reversing) with electric headlamp, first-class compartment coach and brake-third coach, both fitted for electric lighting, twelve EA2 Curved Rails, and a Terminal Connecting Plate. Space required—4 ft. 6 in. square. Supplied in the standard colours of the London Metropolitan Line.   Price 57/6

CLOCKWORK

No. 3C (Clockwork). Locomotive (reversing), first-class compartment coach, brake-third coach, twelve A2 Curved Rails, three B1 Straight Rails and a BBR1 Brake and Reverse Rail by means of which the Train can be either braked or reversed from the track. Space required—6 ft. 3 in. by 4 ft. 6 in.   Price 40/-

The components of the Metropolitan Train Sets can be obtained separately. For prices see pages 31 and 36.

HORNBY *Metropolitan* TRAIN SETS

HORNBY E220 ELECTRIC and No. 2 CLOCKWORK
TANK PASSENGER TRAIN SETS
L.M.S., L.N.E.R., G.W.R. or S.R.

Gauge O, 1¼ in.

*No. 2 Clockwork Tank
Passenger Train Set, L.M.S.*

20-VOLT ELECTRIC—AUTOMATIC REVERSING
E220 (20-volt). Tank Locomotive (automatic reversing) with electric headlamp, one first-third No. 2 Passenger Coach, one brake-third No. 2 Passenger Coach, twelve EA2 Curved Rails, two EB1 Straight Rails, and a Terminal Connecting Plate. Space required—5 ft. 4 in. by 4 ft. 6 in.
Price 50/-

CLOCKWORK
No. 2 (Clockwork). Tank Locomotive (reversing), one first-third No. 2 Passenger Coach, one brake-third No. 2 Passenger Coach, twelve A2 Curved Rails, one B1 Straight Rail and one BBR Straight Brake and Reverse Rail by means of which the Train can be either braked or reversed from the track. Space required—5 ft. 4 in. by 4 ft. 6 in. Price 37/6

The components of the above Passenger Train Sets are obtainable separately at the following prices:—
E220 Special Electric Tank Locomotive (20-volt) automatic reversing	Price 30/-
No. 2 Special Clockwork Tank Locomotive, reversing	Price 19/6
No. 2 Passenger Coach, first-third	Price 6/6
No. 2 Passenger Coach, brake-third	Price 6/6

HORNBY E220 ELECTRIC TANK and No. 2 CLOCKWORK
TANK MIXED GOODS TRAIN SETS
L.M.S., L.N.E.R., G.W.R. or S.R.

*No. 2 Clockwork
Tank Mixed Goods
Train Set, G.W.R.*

20-VOLT ELECTRIC—AUTOMATIC REVERSING
E220 (20-volt). Tank Locomotive (automatic reversing) with electric headlamp, No. 1 Wagon, No. 1 Cattle Truck, Oil Tank Wagon, Brake Van, twelve EA2 Rails, two EB1 Straight Rails and a Terminal Connecting Plate. Space required—5 ft. 4 in. by 4 ft. 6 in. Price 45/-

CLOCKWORK
No. 2 (Clockwork). Tank Locomotive (reversing), No. 1 Wagon, No. 1 Cattle Truck, Oil Tank Wagon, Brake Van, twelve A2 Curved Rails, one B1 Straight Rail and a BBR Straight Brake and Reverse Rail by means of which the Train can be either braked or reversed from the track. Space required—5 ft. 4 in. by 4 ft. 6 in. Price 32/6

The components of the above Goods Train Sets are obtainable separately at the following prices:—
E220 Special Electric Tank Locomotive (20-volt) automatic reversing.	Price 30/-
No. 2 Special Clockwork Tank Locomotive, reversing	Price 19/6
Oil Tank Wagon ... Price 1/11	No. 1 Cattle Truck Price 2/3
No. 1 Wagon ... Price 1/6	Brake Van ... Price 2/9

If you are interested in Deferred Payment Terms turn to page 49.

The prices of Hornby Rails, Points and Crossings are given in pages 49, 50 and 51. For particulars and prices of Transformers, see page 34

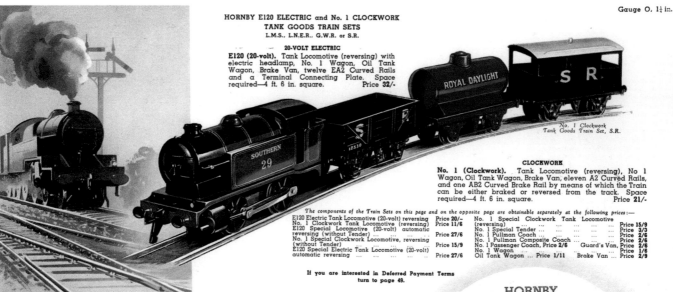

Gauge O, 1¼ in.

HORNBY E120 ELECTRIC and No. 1 CLOCKWORK
TANK GOODS TRAIN SETS
L.M.S., L.N.E.R., G.W.R. or S.R.

20-VOLT ELECTRIC
E120 (20-volt). Tank Locomotive (reversing) with electric headlamp, No. 1 Wagon, Oil Tank Wagon, Brake Van, twelve EA2 Curved Rails and a Terminal Connecting Plate. Space required—4 ft. 6 in. square. Price 32/-

*No. 1 Clockwork
Tank Goods Train Set, S.R.*

CLOCKWORK
No. 1 (Clockwork). Tank Locomotive (reversing), No 1 Wagon, Oil Tank Wagon, Brake Van, eleven A2 Curved Rails, and one AB2 Curved Brake Rail by means of which the Train can be either braked or reversed from the track. Space required—4 ft. 6 in. square. Price 21/-

The components of the Train Sets on this page and on the opposite page are obtainable separately at the following prices:—
E120 Electric Tank Locomotive (20-volt) reversing	Price 20/-	No. 1 Special Clockwork Tank Locomotive (reversing)	Price 15/9
No. 1 Clockwork Tank Locomotive (reversing)	Price 11/6	No. 1 Special Tender	Price 3/3
E120 Special Locomotive (20-volt) automatic reversing (without Tender)	Price 27/6	No. 1 Pullman Coach	Price 2/6
No. 1 Special Clockwork Locomotive, reversing (without Tender)	Price 15/9	No. 1 Pullman Composite Coach	Price 2/6
E120 Special Electric Tank Locomotive (20-volt) automatic reversing	Price 27/6	No. 1 Passenger Coach, Price 2/6 Guard's Van,	Price 2/6
		No. 1 Wagon	Price 1/6
		Oil Tank Wagon ... Price 1/11 Brake Van ...	Price 2/9

If you are interested in Deferred Payment Terms turn to page 49.

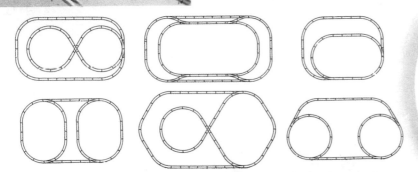

HORNBY
RAIL FORMATIONS

There is practically no limit to the number of rail formations that can be built with Hornby Rails, Points and Crossings. The examples shown in the accompanying illustrations are six of a large variety illustrated and described in the booklet "Hornby Layouts—One Hundred Suggestions", which is obtainable from your dealer, price 3d., or direct from Meccano Limited, Binns Road, Liverpool 13, price 4d., post free. The purpose of this book is to show how the wide range of Hornby Rails, Points and Crossings can be employed in the assembly of clockwork and electric layouts of all kinds, from simple designs to the most elaborate formations. The Hornby Railway System is constructed to Gauge O, the most popular of all standard gauges for miniature railways. In this gauge the track is 1¼ in. wide, the measurement being made between the insides of the heads of the rails.

The prices of Hornby Rails, Points and Crossings, both electric and clockwork, are given in pages 49, 50 and 51.

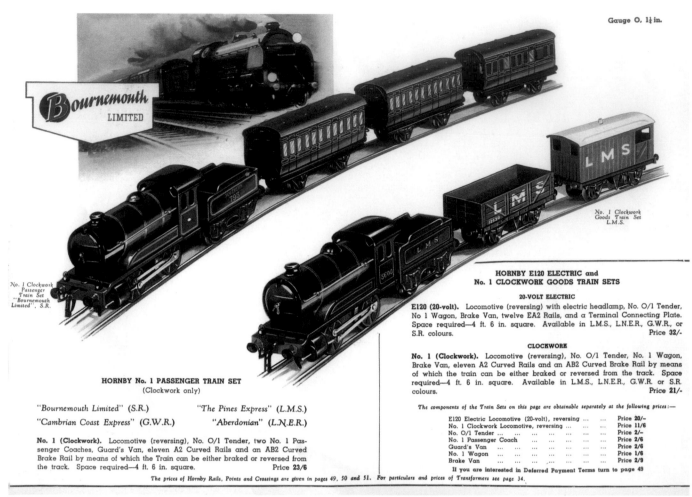

Gauge O, 1¼ in.

Bournemouth LIMITED

No. 1 Clockwork Goods Train Set L.M.S.

No. 1 Clockwork Passenger Train Set "Bournemouth Limited", S.R.

HORNBY E120 ELECTRIC and
No. 1 CLOCKWORK GOODS TRAIN SETS

20-VOLT ELECTRIC

E120 (20-volt). Locomotive (reversing) with electric headlamp, No. O/1 Tender, No 1 Wagon, Brake Van, twelve EA2 Rails, and a Terminal Connecting Plate. Space required—4 ft. 6 in. square. Available in L.M.S., L.N.E.R., G.W.R., or S.R. colours.   Price 32/-

CLOCKWORK

No. 1 (Clockwork). Locomotive (reversing), No. O/1 Tender, No. 1 Wagon, Brake Van, eleven A2 Curved Rails and an AB2 Curved Brake Rail by means of which the train can be either braked or reversed from the track. Space required—4 ft. 6 in. square. Available in L.M.S., L.N.E.R., G.W.R. or S.R. colours.   Price 21/-

HORNBY No. 1 PASSENGER TRAIN SET
(Clockwork only)

"Bournemouth Limited" (S.R.)   "The Pines Express" (L.M.S.)

"Cambrian Coast Express" (G.W.R.)   "Aberdonian" (L.N.E.R.)

No. 1 (Clockwork). Locomotive (reversing), No. O/1 Tender, two No. 1 Passenger Coaches, Guard's Van, eleven A2 Curved Rails and an AB2 Curved Brake Rail by means of which the train can be either braked or reversed from the track. Space required—4 ft. 6 in. square.   Price 23/6

The components of the Train Sets on this page are obtainable separately at the following prices:—

E120 Electric Locomotive (20-volt), reversing	Price 20/-
No. 1 Clockwork Locomotive, reversing	Price 11/6
No. O/1 Tender	Price 2/-
No. 1 Passenger Coach	Price 2/6
Guard's Van	Price 2/6
No. 1 Wagon	Price 1/6
Brake Van	Price 2/9

If you are interested in Deferred Payment Terms turn to page 49

The prices of Hornby Rails, Points and Crossings are given in pages 49, 50 and 51. For particulars and prices of Transformers see page 34.

THE COMET
(L.M.S.)

Gauge O, 1¼ in.

HORNBY E120 SPECIAL ELECTRIC and No. 1 SPECIAL CLOCKWORK PASSENGER TRAIN SETS

No. 1 Special Clockwork Passenger Train Set, L.M.S.

20-VOLT ELECTRIC—AUTOMATIC REVERSING
E120 Special (20-volt). Locomotive (automatic reversing) with electric headlamp, No. 1 Special Tender, two No. 1 Pullman Coaches and one No. 1 Pullman Composite Coach for L.N.E.R. and S.R., or two No. 1 Passenger Coaches and a Guard's Van for L.M.S. and G.W.R., twelve EA2 Curved Rails, two EB1 Straight Rails and a Terminal Connecting Plate. Space required—5 ft. 4 in. by 4 ft. 6 in.   Price 45/-

CLOCKWORK
No. 1 Special (Clockwork). Locomotive (reversing) No. 1 Special Tender, two No. 1 Pullman Coaches and one No. 1 Pullman Composite Coach for L.N.E.R. and S.R., or two No. 1 Passenger Coaches and Guard's Van for L.M.S. and G.W.R., twelve A2 Curved Rails, one B1 Straight Rail and one BBR Straight Brake and Reverse Rail by means of which the Train can be either braked or reversed from the track. Space required—5 ft. 4 in. by 4 ft. 6 in.   Price 31/-

"The Comet" (L.M.S.)
(Illustrated above)

"Queen of Scots" (L.N.E.R.)

"Torbay Express" (G.W.R.)

"Bournemouth Belle" (S.R.)

The components of these Train Sets can be purchased separately. For prices see opposite page.

No. 1 Special Clockwork Tank Goods Train Set, L.N.E.R.

HORNBY
E120 SPECIAL ELECTRIC
and No. 1 SPECIAL CLOCKWORK
TANK GOODS TRAIN SETS
L.M.S., L.N.E.R., G.W.R. or S.R.

20-VOLT ELECTRIC—AUTOMATIC REVERSING
E120 Special Tank (20-volt). Tank Locomotive (automatic reversing) with electric headlamp, No. 1 Wagon, Oil Tank Wagon, Brake Van, twelve EA2 Curved Rails, two EB1 Straight Rails and a Terminal Connecting Plate. Space required—5 ft. 4 in. by 4 ft. 6 in.   Price 40/-

CLOCKWORK
No. 1 Special Tank (Clockwork). Tank Locomotive (reversing), No. 1 Wagon, Oil Tank Wagon, Brake Van, twelve A2 Curved Rails, one B1 Straight Rail and one BBR Brake and Reverse Rail by means of which the Train can be either braked or reversed from the track. Space required—5 ft. 4 in. by 4 ft. 6 in.   Price 26/-

HORNBY EO20 ELECTRIC and No. O CLOCKWORK PASSENGER TRAIN SETS

Gauge O, 1¼ in.

EO20 Electric Passenger Train Set

20-VOLT ELECTRIC

EO20 (20-volt). Locomotive (reversing) with electric headlamp, No. O/1 Tender, two No. O Pullman Coaches, six EA1 Curved Rails, two EB1 Straight Rails and one Terminal Connecting Plate. Space required—3 ft. 3 in. by 2 ft. 6 in. Available with Locomotive and Tender in L.M.S., L.N.E.R., G.W.R. or S.R. colours.   Price 27/-

CLOCKWORK

No. O (Clockwork). Locomotive (reversing), No. O/1 Tender, two No. O Pullman Coaches, six A1 Curved Rails, one B1 Straight Rail and one BB1 Straight Brake Rail by means of which the Train can be braked from the track. Space required—3ft. 3in. by 2 ft. 6 in. Available with Locomotive and Tender in L.M.S., L.N.E.R., G.W.R. or S.R. colours   Price 15/9

The components of the Train Sets on this page are obtainable separately at the following prices:—

EO20 Electric Locomotive, (20-volt reversing), (without Tender) ... Price 19/-
No. O/1 Tender, Price 2/-   No. O Pullman Coach, Price 1/3

No. O Clockwork Locomotive, reversing (without Tender) ... ... Price 8/11
No. O Wagon, Price 1/3   No. 1 Timber Wagon, Price 1/3

The prices of Hornby Rails, Points and Crossings are given in pages 49, 50 and 51. For particulars and prices of Transformers see page 34.

HORNBY No. O GOODS TRAIN SET
(Clockwork only)

No. O (Clockwork). Locomotive (reversing), No. O/1 Tender, No. O Wagon, No. 1 Timber Wagon, six A1 Curved Rails, one B1 Straight Rail and one BB1 Straight Brake Rail by means of which the Train can be braked from the track. Space required—3 ft. 3 in. by 2 ft. 6 in. Available with Locomotive, Tender and Wagon in L.M.S., L.N.E.R., G.W.R. or S.R. colours.   Price 15/9

The components of No. O Goods Train Set can be purchased separately. For prices see above.

Gauge O, 1¼ in.   EM320 and EM36 ELECTRIC and M3 CLOCKWORK TANK GOODS TRAIN SETS

EM36 Electric Tank Goods Train Set

20-VOLT AND 6-VOLT ELECTRIC

EM320 (20-volt). Tank Locomotive (reversing) with electric headlamp, available in L.M.S., L.N.E.R., G.W.R. or S.R. colours, one Goods Wagon, one Timber Wagon, one "Royal Daylight" Oil Tank Wagon (not "Shell" as shown in illustration), six EA1 Curved Rails, two EB1 Straight Rails and one Terminal Connecting Plate. Space required—3 ft. 3 in. by 2 ft. 6 in.   Price 24/-

EM36 (6-volt). This Set is similar to the EM320 Set except that the locomotive is fitted with a 6-volt motor.   Price 24/-

CLOCKWORK

M3 (Clockwork). Tank Locomotive (reversing), available in L.M.S., L.N.E.R., G.W.R. or S.R. colours, one Goods Wagon, one Timber Wagon, one "Royal Daylight" Oil Tank Wagon (not "Shell" as shown in illustration), six A1 Curved Rails, three B1 Straight Rails, and one BB1 Straight Brake Rail by means of which the Train can be braked from the track. Space required—4 ft. 3 in. by 2 ft. 6 in.   Price 15/-

M3 TANK PASSENGER TRAIN SET
(Clockwork only)

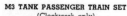

Tank locomotive (reversing) available in L.M.S., L.N.E.R., G.W.R. or S.R. colours, three No. O Pullman Coaches, six A1 Curved Rails, three B1 Straight Rails and one BB1 Straight Brake Rail by means of which the Train can be braked from the track. Space required—4 ft. 3 in. by 2 ft. 6 in.   Price 13/9

The Locomotives in the Train Sets on this page, and the No. O Pullman Coaches of the M3 Clockwork Passenger Train Set, are obtainable separately at the following prices:—

EM320 or EM36 Electric Tank Locomotive (reversible from cab) ... . Price 16/6
M3 Clockwork Tank Locomotive (reversing) ... ... Price 7/6
No. O Pullman Coach ... ... Price 1/3

The prices of Hornby Rails, Points and Crossings are given in pages 49, 50 and 51. For particulars and prices of Transformers see page 34.

EM120 and EM16 ELECTRIC and M1 CLOCKWORK GOODS TRAIN SETS

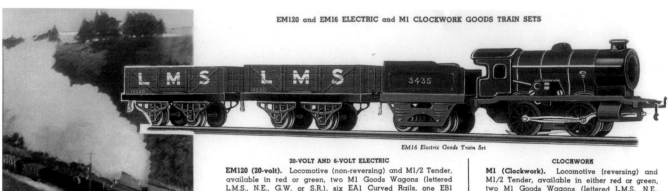

EM16 Electric Goods Train Set

20-VOLT AND 6-VOLT ELECTRIC

EM120 (20-volt). Locomotive (non-reversing) and M1/2 Tender, available in red or green, two M1 Goods Wagons (lettered L.M.S., N.E., G.W. or S.R.), six EA1 Curved Rails, one EB1 Straight Rail and one EMC20 Switch Rail by means of which the train can be started or stopped.   Space required—3 ft. 3 in. by 2 ft. 6 in.   Price 15/-

EM16 (6-volt).   This Set is similar to the EM120 Set except that the locomotive is fitted with a 6-volt motor.   Price 15/-

CLOCKWORK

M1 (Clockwork).   Locomotive (reversing) and M1/2 Tender, available in either red or green, two M1 Goods Wagons (lettered L.M.S., N.E., G.W. or S.R.), six A1 Curved Rails, one B1 Straight Rail and one BB1 Straight Brake Rail by means of which the Train can be braked from the track.   Space required—3 ft. 3 in. by 2 ft. 6 in.   Price 8/11

EM120 ELECTRIC and M1 and M2 CLOCKWORK PASSENGER TRAIN SETS

EM120 Electric Passenger Train Set

20-VOLT ELECTRIC

EM120 (20-volt). Locomotive (non-reversing) and M1/2 Tender, available in red or green, two M1 Pullman Coaches, six EA1 Curved Rails, one EB1 Straight Rail and one EMC20 Switch Rail by means of which the train can be started or stopped.   Space required—3 ft. 3 in. by 2 ft. 6 in.
Price 15/-

CLOCKWORK

M1 (Clockwork).   Locomotive (reversing) and M1/2 Tender, available in either red or green, two M1 Pullman Coaches, six A1 Curved Rails, one B1 Straight Rail and one BB1 Straight Brake Rail by means of which the Train can be braked from the track.   Space required—3 ft. 3 in. by 2 ft. 6 in.   Price 8/11

M2 (Clockwork).   This Set is similar to the M1 Clockwork Passenger Set except that it has three M1 Pullman Coaches and two extra B1 Straight Rails.   Space required—4 ft. 3 in. by 2 ft. 6 in.   Price 10/6

The components of the Train Sets on this page are obtainable separately at the following prices:—

EM120 or EM16 Electric Locomotive, non-reversing (without Tender)	Price 8/6
M1/2 Clockwork Locomotive, reversing (without Tender), for M1 and M2 Clockwork Train Sets	Price 4/6
M1 Wagon ... ... Price 10d.   M1/2 Tender ... ... Price 9d.   M1 Pullman Coach ... Price 1/-

The prices of Hornby Rails, Points and Crossings are given in pages 49, 50 and 51. For particulars and prices of Transformers see page 34.

No. O "SILVER JUBILEE" TRAIN SET, L.N.E.R.
(Clockwork only)

Streamline Locomotive "Silver Link" (non-reversing) and Tender, Articulated Saloon Coach, five M9 Curved Rails and an MB9 Curved Brake Rail by means of which the train can be braked from the track.   Space required—2 ft. square.   Price 7/6

No. O STREAMLINE TRAIN SET (Clockwork only)

Similar in design to, and having the same contents as, the No. O "Silver Jubilee" Train Set, illustrated and described above.   Finished in two different colour schemes, maroon/cream and light green/dark green, and without lettering.   Price 7/6

The components of the above train sets are obtainable separately at the following prices:—

No. O "Silver Link" Clockwork Locomotive, non-reversing (without Tender)	Price 3/6
No. O Streamline Locomotive, non-reversing (without Tender)	Price 3/6
No. O "Silver Link" Tender	Price 1/-
No. O "Silver Jubilee" Articulated Saloon Coach	Price 1/9
No. O Streamline Tender	Price 1/-
No. O Streamline Articulated Saloon Coach	Price 1/9

MO MIXED
GOODS TRAIN SET
(Clockwork only)

Locomotive (non-reversing) and Tender, available in either red or green, Side Tipping Wagon, Rotary Tipping Wagon, Petrol Tank Wagon, five M9 Curved Rails, two BM Straight Rails, and an MB9 Curved Brake Rail.   Space required—2 ft. 9 in. by 2 ft.   Price 6/11

The components of the above Train Set can be purchased separately. For prices see opposite page.

Gauge O, 1¼ in.

MO PASSENGER TRAIN SET
(Clockwork only)

Locomotive (non-reversing) and Tender, available in red or green, two Pullman Coaches, five M9 Curved Rails and an MB9 Curved Brake Rail by means of which the train can be braked from the track. Space required—2 ft. square. Price **5/6**

MO GOODS TRAIN SET
(Clockwork only)

Locomotive (non-reversing) and Tender, available in red or green, two wagons, five M9 Curved Rails and an MB9 Curved Brake Rail by means of which the train can be braked from the track. Space required—2 ft. square. Price **4/11**

The components of the MO Passenger and Goods Train Sets can be purchased separately at the following prices:—

MO Locomotive, non-reversing (without Tender) Price **2/9**	MO Tender ... ... Price **6d.**	MO Petrol Tank Wagon ... ... Price **1/-**
MO Pullman Coach ... ... Price **9d.**	MO Wagon ... ... Price **6d.**	MO Rotary Tipping Wagon ... ... Price **1/-**
MO Side Tipping Wagon... ... ... Price **1/-**		

For prices of MO Rails and Points (9 in. radius) see page 51

HORNBY PART EXCHANGE SCHEME

NEW HORNBY LOCOMOTIVES FOR OLD

This is the finest part exchange offer ever made. You have probably been using a Hornby Locomotive for some years and would now like to own one of the latest electric or clockwork models featured on pages 30 and 31 of this catalogue. The object of the Hornby Locomotive Part Exchange Scheme is to help you to do this.

The allowance that will be made for your old Locomotive is shown in a special list of Part Exchange allowances for Hornby Locomotives obtainable from your dealer. Please note that the catalogue price of the new Hornby Locomotive you purchase must not be less than double the Part Exchange allowance made for your old Locomotive.

No matter what its age or condition your old Locomotive can be exchanged under our "Part Exchange" plan. It is important to note that we cannot accept more than one old Locomotive in exchange for one new Locomotive.

WHAT YOU HAVE TO DO

Here is an example of how the plan works. Assuming you have a No. 1 Tank Locomotive that you wish to exchange, you see from the list that its exchange value is 5/9. You then choose a new Locomotive, the cost of which is not less than 11/6 (or, in other words, not less than double the Part Exchange allowance we make for your No. 1 Tank Locomotive).

You decide, say, to have a No. 2 Special Tank Locomotive, the price of which is **19/6**. Pack up your old No. 1 Tank, take it to your dealer with a remittance for **13/9**, and he will exchange it for the new model that you require.

The Hornby Railway System includes a complete range of Rolling Stock, Accessories, and Rails, Points and Crossings, with which the most elaborate model railway can be constructed. Every component in the Hornby Series is well designed and carefully modelled on its prototype.

Hornby Rolling Stock includes almost every type in use on the big railways. Special attention is directed to the new Corridor Coaches shown on this page. These splendid models include in their design all the features characteristic of the latest main line stock of the four groups.

The Accessories are now better than ever before, while the Rails, Points and Crossings allow an endless variety of layouts to be contructed.

No. 2 CORRIDOR COACH L.M.S. (First-Third)
A perfect model of a modern side corridor coach with end doors. Not suitable for 1 ft. radius rails.
Price **7/6**

No. 2 CORRIDOR COACH L.M.S. (Brake Composite)
A realistic vehicle reproducing the latest standard steel-panelled stock. Not suitable for 1 ft. radius rails.
Price **7/6**

No. 2 CORRIDOR COACH L.N.E.R. (First-Third)
A handsome coach finished to represent the varnished teak stock of the L.N.E.R. Not suitable for 1 ft. radius rails.
Price **7/6**

No. 2 CORRIDOR COACH G.W.R. (First-Third)
The design of this coach is based on the latest corridor stock built for general main line service on the G.W.R. Not suitable for 1 ft. radius rails. Price **7/6**

No. 2 CORRIDOR COACH S.R. (Third Class)
A model of the latest type "open third" centre-corridor coaches recently introduced on the S.R. Not suitable for 1 ft. radius rails.
Price **7/6**

No. 2 CORRIDOR COACH L.N.E.R. (Brake Composite)
This coach has guard's and luggage compartments at one end and is a necessary vehicle to complete any miniature L.N.E.R. express train. Not suitable for 1 ft. radius rails. Price **7/6**

No. 2 CORRIDOR COACH G.W.R. (Brake Composite)
This follows the typical G.W.R. arrangement of brake composite coaches, with the guard's compartment between the passenger and the luggage portions. Not suitable for 1 ft. radius rails. Price **7/6**

No. 2 CORRIDOR COACH S.R. (Brake Composite)
A well-proportioned vehicle modelled on the standard side corridor coaches built for S.R. steam-worked main line services. Not suitable for 1 ft. radius rails. Price **7/6**

HORNBY ROLLING STOCK
FITTED WITH AUTOMATIC COUPLINGS

No. 2 PASSENGER COACH (First/Third)
Available in correct colours of L.M.S., L.N.E., G.W. or Southern Railway Companies' rolling stock. Not suitable for 1 ft. radius rails. Price 6/6

No. 2 PASSENGER COACH (Brake/Composite)
Available in correct colours of L.M.S., L.N.E., G.W. or Southern Railway Companies' rolling stock. Not suitable for 1 ft. radius rails. Price 6/6

No. 2 SALOON COACH
Finished in the colours of the L.N.E. (as illustrated) or L.M.S. Railway Companies. Not suitable for 1 ft. radius rails. Price 9/6

RIVIERA "BLUE" TRAIN COACH
"Dining Car" or "Sleeping Car". Not suitable for 1 ft. radius rails. Price 10/6

CONTINENTAL "MITROPA" COACH No. 3
Similar in design to the Riviera "Blue" Train Coach. Finished in red, with white roof, and lettered "Mitropa" in gold. Price 10/6

No. 2 SPECIAL PULLMAN COACH
This coach is perfect in detail and finish. Lettered "Loraine", "Zenobia" and "Grosvenor". Not suitable for 1 ft. radius rails. Price 13/-

No. 2 SPECIAL PULLMAN COACH COMPOSITE
One part is designed for passenger accommodation and the other for luggage. Lettered "Verona", "Alberta" and "Montana". Not suitable for 1 ft. radius rails. Price 13/-

No. 2 PULLMAN COACH
Not suitable for 1 ft. radius rails. Price 9/6

METROPOLITAN COACH C
First class or brake-third. Not suitable for 1 ft. radius rails. Price 7/6

METROPOLITAN COACH E
First class or brake-third. Fitted for electric lighting. Not suitable for 1 ft. radius rails. Price 11/6

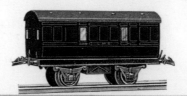

No. O "SILVER JUBILEE" ARTICULATED SALOON COACH
This is an interesting model of the type of coach used with the "Silver Jubilee" Train. Finished in silver and grey. Price 1/9

No. O STREAMLINE ARTICULATED SALOON COACH
Finished in maroon/cream or light green/dark green. Price 1/9

PULLMAN CAR
American Type (as illustrated) Yellow or green with orange or red roof. Lettered "Washington" or "Madison" Price 1/6
Continental Type. "Mitropa" No. O. Red with white roof. Lettered "Mitropa". Price 1/6

M1/2 PULLMAN COACH
Named "Marjorie", "Aurelia" or "Viking" Price 1/-
No. O PULLMAN COACH
Similar to M1 Pullman Coach, illustrated above, but fitted with automatic couplings. Price 1/3

No. 1 PASSENGER COACH
Available in correct colours of L.M.S., L.N.ER., G.W.R. or S.R. Price 2/6

GUARD'S VAN
Available in correct colours of L.M.S., L.N.ER., G.W.R. or S.R. Price 2/6

MO PULLMAN COACH
As supplied with MO Passenger Set. Available named "Joan" or "Zena". (MO coupling) Price 9d.

No. 1 PULLMAN COACH
Distinctive in design and beautifully finished. Named "Cynthia", "Corsair" and "Niobe". Price 2/6

No. 1 PULLMAN COACH COMPOSITE
One part of this coach is designed for passenger accommodation and the other for conveyance of luggage. Named "Ansonia" or "Aurora". Price 2/6

CABOOSE (American)
This is a realistic model of the type of brake van used on the American railroads. Price 2/-

No. 1 CATTLE TRUCK
Fitted with sliding doors. Available lettered L.M.S., N.E., G.W. or S.R. Price 2/3

No. 2 CATTLE TRUCK
Bogie model fitted with double doors. Not suitable for 1 ft. radius rails. Available lettered L.M.S., N.E., G.W. or S.R. Price 4/6

BOX CAR (American Type)
A realistic model of the type of vehicle used in America for the conveyance of luggage and perishables. Price 2/3

HORNBY DUBLO

SUPER-DETAIL

2-RAIL

TRAIN SETS

Power Control units are NOT included in these Train Sets. Your local dealer will be pleased to advise the most suitable unit for your purpose.

NEW

Page 8

From a post-war Hornby Dublo catalogue

THE RIGHT ENGINE FOR EVERY JOB IN HORNBY-DUBLO

Co-Co Type Diesel-Electric Locomotive
This engine is based on a powerful Co-Co diesel-electric design by the English Electric Company Limited for heavy main line service on British Railways.
2232 Co-Co Diesel-Electric Locomotive (2-rail).
3232 Co-Co Diesel-Electric Locomotive (3-rail).
Price £4.2.6 each

"Golden Fleece" 4-6-2 Locomotive and Tender
A special favourite with East Coast route enthusiasts. Represents the streamlined A4 Pacifics still in active use on fast and heavy long-distance expresses.
2211 "Golden Fleece" and Tender E.R. (2-rail).
3211 "Mallard" and Tender E.R. (3-rail).
Price £3.19.6 each

0-6-2 Tank Locomotive
A popular and hard-working locomotive, well known since the Hornby-Dublo system began. Useful for passenger or goods trains.
2217 0-6-2 Tank Locomotive (2-rail).
3217 0-6-2 Tank Locomotive (3-rail).
Price £2.12.6 each

NEW

2-6-4 Tank Locomotive
A reproduction of the B.R. Standard class 4 tank locomotive for passenger and goods duties.
2218 2-6-4 Tank Locomotive B.R. (2-rail).
3218 2-6-4 Tank Locomotive B.R. (3-rail).
Price £3.12.6 each

"Cardiff Castle" 4-6-0 Locomotive and Tender
This is the latest version in Hornby-Dublo of one of the most famous steam locomotives, the Western Region Castle Class 4-6-0.
2221 "Cardiff Castle" and Tender (2-rail).
3221 "Ludlow Castle" and Tender (3-rail).
Price £4.4.0 each

Co-Bo type Diesel-Electric Locomotive
A well-detailed diesel with an unusual wheel arrangement. It reproduces the Type 2 1200 h.p. locomotives built by Metropolitan-Vickers.
2233 Co-Bo Diesel-Electric Locomotive (2-rail).
3233 Co-Bo Diesel-Electric Locomotive (3-rail).
Price £4.2.6 each

Page 10

★*Fitted with the famous Ring Field Motor*

. . . FOR 2-RAIL AND 3-RAIL SYSTEMS

★   ★   NEW

2-8-0 8F Locomotive and Tender
A Locomotive of workmanlike design specially suitable for heavy freight traffic on Hornby-Dublo railways.
2224 2-8-0 8F Goods Locomotive and Tender (2-rail).
3224 2-8-0 8F Goods Locomotive and Tender (3-rail).
Price £4.6.6 each

Rebuilt West Country Class 4-6-2 Locomotive and Tender
The latest steam type locomotive in Hornby-Dublo. It reproduces the characteristic features of a popular class well known on Southern routes.
2235 4-6-2 S.R. West Country Locomotive "Barnstaple" and Tender (2-rail).
3235 4-6-2 S.R. West Country Locomotive "Dorchester" and Tender (3-rail).
Price £5.15.0 each

0-6-0 Tank Locomotive
An attractive engine of familiar outline, useful on any 2-rail layout. Easily placed on the track by the beginner.
2207 0-6-0 Tank Locomotive (Green) (2-rail only).
2206 0-6-0 Tank Locomotive B.R. (Black) (2-rail only).
Price £1.16.0 each

★

"City of London" Locomotive and Tender
The maroon livery gives this engine an air of distinction. The real "City of London" belongs to the well known L.M.R. Coronation Class.
2226 "City of London" and Tender L.M.R. (2-rail).
3226 "City of Liverpool" and Tender L.M.R. (3-rail).
Price £4.9.0 each

0-6-0 Diesel-Electric Shunting Locomotive
This is a realistic representation of the B.R. Standard Diesel-Electric Shunting Locomotives of which there are now over 1,000 in service.
2231 0-6-0 Diesel-Electric Shunting Locomotive (2-rail).
3231 0-6-0 Diesel-Electric Shunting Locomotive (3-rail).
Price £2.18.6 each

Bo-Bo Diesel-Electric Locomotive and Tender
A distinctive reproduction in miniature of the first B.R. Standard class of diesel for main line duties. It is very fully detailed.
2230 1,000 b.h.p. Bo-Bo Diesel Electric Locomotive (2-rail).
3230 1,000 b.h.p. Bo-Bo Diesel Electric Locomotive (3-rail).
Price £3.1.0 each

Page 11

Set No. 2008 0-6-0 TANK GOODS TRAIN, (for 2-rail track) comprising 0-6-0 Tank Locomotive (Black), U.G.B. Sand Wagon, Goods Wagon (Steel Type), Goods Brake Van W.R., and two-rail track requiring a space 3 ft. by 3 ft.
Price £3.5.0

OTHER TRAIN SETS NOT ILLUSTRATED

Set No. 2006 0-6-0 TANK GOODS TRAIN (for 2-rail track). As Set No. 2008 but with Green Tank Locomotive.
Price £3.5.0

Set No. 2009 0-6-0 TANK PASSENGER TRAIN (for 2-rail track). As Set No. 2007 but with Black Tank Locomotive and Maroon coaches.
Price £3.18.6

Set No. 2016 0-6-2 TANK GOODS TRAIN, (for 2-rail track) comprising 0-6-2 Tank Locomotive, "SAXA SALT" Wagon, "MOBIL" Tank Wagon, Low-sided Wagon with two Cable Drums, Goods Brake Van, L.M.R. and two-rail track requiring a space of 4 ft. by 3 ft.
Price £4.19.6

PULLMAN CARS — ROLLING STOCK for 2-rail and 3-rail systems

4035
Pullman Car 1st Class with Interior Fittings. Overall length 9¾ in.
18/6

4036
Pullman Car 2nd Class with Interior Fittings. Overall length 9¾ in.
18/6

4037
Pullman Car Brake/2nd with Interior Fittings. Overall length 9¾ in.
18/6

4652
Machine Wagon LOWMAC.
Length 5½ in.
7/-

4626
PRESFLO Bulk Cement Wagon B.R. Length 3½ in.
7/-

4627
I.C.I. 20-ton Bulk Salt Wagon. Length 3½ in.
7/-

4300
"Blue Spot" Fish Van E.R. Length 4⅜ in.
6/9

4323
S.R. 4-Wheeled Utility Van. Length 5⅛ in.
12/6

DUBLO DINKY TOYS ADD REALISM TO ANY LAYOUT

073
Land Rover (with windows) and Horse Trailer (with Horse). Length 4⅜ in.
4/3

070
A.E.C. Mercury Tanker SHELL B.P. (with windows). Length 3⅜ in.
2/6

067
Austin Taxi. Length 2⅜ in.
2/6

076
Lansing Bagnall Tractor and Trailer. Length 2⅞ in.
2/9

078
Lansing Bagnall Trailer only. Length 1⅜ in.
1/6

DUBLO DINKY TOYS
Made to the scale of 'oo' gauge trains.

050 Railway Staff (HO/OO)		
	Set of 12	3/-
052 Railway Passengers (HO/OO)		
	available later	
064 Austin Lorry		1/6
067 Austin Taxi		2/6
068 Royal Mail Van (with windows)		2/3
069 Massey-Harris Ferguson Tractor		1/6
070 A.E.C. Mercury Tanker Shell-BP (with windows)		2/6
071 Volkswagen Delivery Van Hornby - Dublo (with windows)		2/-
072 Bedford Articulated Flat Truck (with windows) ..		2/6
073 Land Rover (with windows) & Horse Trailer (with horse)		4/3
076 Lansing Bagnall Tractor and Trailer		2/9
078 Lansing Bagnall Trailer only		1/6

Page 15

Gauge OO—⅝ in.

NEW

HORNBY DUBLO

OPEN COACHES WITH INTERIOR FITTINGS for 2-rail and 3-rail systems

All seven coaches and five items of rolling stock on this and the opposite page are authentic models, bringing variety and colour to Hornby-Dublo railways. The Pullman Cars are particularly attractive with moulded bodies and bases and detailed interiors.

4062
Open Coach 1st Class B.R. with Interior Fittings. Length 9¾ in.
16/-

4061
Open Coach 2nd Class W.R. with Interior Fittings. Length 9¾ in.
16/-

4060
Open Coach 1st Class W.R. with Interior Fittings. Length 9¾ in.
16/-

4063
Open Coach 2nd Class B.R. with Interior Fittings. Length 9¾ in.
16/-

INTERIOR FITTINGS
The latest Hornby-Dublo Corridor Coaches, based on B.R. Standard designs, have interiors representing the seating and the corridor partitions. In the Sleeping Car even the individual berths are included.

Tri-ang WRENN HEAVY DIE-CAST METAL LOCOMOTIVES

These superb heavy locomotives, decorated in a selection of British Railways colours and those of the four famous Railway Companies, have fine body detailing, individual handrails and nickel tyres on their driving wheels. Operating from 12 volts D.C. they are each fitted with a Tri-ang Hornby coupling.

W.2227 520
4-6-2 PRINCESS
CORONATION CLASS 8P
LOCOMOTIVE "CITY OF STOKE-ON-TRENT"
with tender, in L.M.S. colours.

W.2226 520
4-6-2 PRINCESS
CORONATION CLASS 8P
LOCOMOTIVE "CITY OF LONDON"
with tender, in B.R. colours.

W.2212 500
4-6-2 CLASS A4
LOCOMOTIVE "SIR NIGEL GRESLEY"
with tender, in L.N.E.R. colours.

W.2211 4-6-2 CLASS A4 500
LOCOMOTIVE "MALLARD"
with tender,
in B.R. colours.

380
W.2217 0-6-2
CLASS N2 TANK
LOCOMOTIVE
in L.N.E.R. colours.

380
W.2216 0-6-2
CLASS N2 TANK
LOCOMOTIVE
in B.R. colours.

From a Tri-ang Hornby catalogue

W.2236 480
4-6-2 WEST COUNTRY CLASS
LOCOMOTIVE "DORCHESTER"
with tender, in B.R. colours.

W.2222 500
4-6-0 CASTLE CLASS
LOCOMOTIVE "DEVIZES CASTLE"
with tender, in G.W.R. colours.

W.2225 500
2-8-0 CLASS 8F
LOCOMOTIVE
with tender, in L.M.S. colours.

480
W.2218 2-6-4 CLASS 4MT
TANK LOCOMOTIVE
in B.R. colours.

Tri-ang HORNBY LOCOMOTIVE KITS AND ACCESSORIES

340
R.388U CLASS EM2 Co-Co LOCOMOTIVE "ELECTRA". Supplied complete with screwdriver, the only tool you need. No previous experience is needed to assemble this model and building it will help you to understand how the locomotive operates and will stimulate your interest in engineering.

440
R.386G 4-6-2 LOCOMOTIVE "THE PRINCESS ROYAL" with crew and tender. Decorated in authentic L.M.S. livery, a choice of three names is included with the locomotive. All motor parts are already wired and pre-soldered. Just assemble, with screwdriver included in the pack.

420
R.396 "HYMEK" B-B DIESEL HYDRAULIC LOCOMOTIVE. The kit includes sufficient finished parts for you to assemble a replica of this modern B.R. diesel locomotive. Fully detailed instructions and screwdriver are included and no expert knowledge is required.

R.413 LOCOMOTIVE CREW. Available for your older locomotives.

R.281 5 TRAIN FIGURES. Driver, Fireman, Motorman and 2 Guards.

R.521 CAPSULE OF SMOKE OIL. Locomotives with Syncrosmoke are supplied complete with one capsule.

R.297U POWER CLEAN BRUSH. Plugs into Super 4 Power Connecting Clip or System 6 Track to make locomotive wheels revolve while brush simultaneously removes dirt.

15
DINKY TOYS

Hornby Modelled Miniatures

Hornby's Modelled Miniatures were intended to be used in conjunction with Hornby trains when they were introduced in 1933 and most of the items in the range were made to a similar scale. In addition to the Sports Coupe, Sports Car, Delivery Van, Motor Truck, Farm Tractor and Army Tank, Frank also made station platforms, a Hall's Distemper Advertisement board, Gradient signs and mile posts, milk churns and trucks to carry them in, luggage and a trolley, station name boards, people, and animals. He even made a miniature die cast train set with a six wheeled tank locomotive, an open wagon, a crane truck and two petrol trucks. The van and the truck shared the same cab and front, while the Sports Coupe with its raised hood and the Sports Car shared nothing in common. In his excellent book *The History of British Dinky Toys 1934–1964* Cecil Gibson pointed out that, of the farm animals, one cow was a Devon Red and another was a British Holstein. The tractor was a Fordson and this exemplifies Frank Hornby's meticulous concern for detail and authenticity which undoubtedly contributed to the success of his products.

Pre-War Dinky Toys

Dinky Toys represented an important progression from Modelled Miniatures and they first appeared in 1934. Hornby already had a base in France and so British and French Dinky Toys developed side by side, but with distinct models, from the beginning.

The very first Dinky Toys were in fact identical to Modelled Miniatures but they were marketed under the new name and numbered from 22a to 22f. They were priced between 6d and one shilling and the set of six vehicles could be purchased for 4 shillings or 20 new pence.

In addition to these models an important new range of vehicles was released in 1934. This included the No. 23 racing car which was modelled on a streamlined MG that raced at Brooklands. It was an inexpensive model that would reappear after the War painted silver with red trim but in the 1930s it was available in a variety of attractive colours.

Then there was the No. 24 range, designated 24a to 24h, consisting of an Ambulance, which was also made after the War, a Limousine, a Town Sedan, a Vogue Saloon, a Super Streamline Saloon, a Sportsman's coupe, a four seater Sports Tourer and a Two seater Sports Tourer. Each of these had a separate base plate which included the mudguards and running boards and they were painted in bright colours to contrast with the colour of the bodies, unlike the base plates of the post-war models which of course were all black. The wheels were smooth instead of ridged and the tyres were often white in colour. As was the case with the reissued models after the War they all had separate silvered die cast radiators and headlamps. The sports cars had tin windscreens and sometimes tiny tinplate drivers.

The 25 Series lorries, of much smaller scale than the cars, were numbered from 25a to 25f and consisted of a Wagon, a Covered Wagon. a Flat Truck, a Petrol Tank wagon, a Tipping Truck and a Market Gardener's van. All of these, apart from the petrol lorry, were very similar but the covered wagon and the petrol tanker came in a variety of colours and logos, making them highly valued today.

The first 28 Series consisted of Delivery Vans, all identical but with a rich variety of colours and logos, including Pickfords, Oxo, Hornby Trains, Meccano and Kodak Film.

Two unusual models in a much smaller scale were a Tram Car and a double decker Motor Bus which had an entrance in the middle of its near side.

Additions to the range in 1935 included No. 31, a Holland Coachcraft van which was remarkably similar to, but much rarer than, the later streamlined coach. No. 22h was a Streamline Saloon which later developed into the larger Chysler Airflow, and an important new range, numbered 33, was based on a three wheeled Mechanical Horse and two wheeled trailer. The trailers consisted of a Flat Truck, an Open Wagon, a Box Van, a Dust Wagon and a Petrol Tanker. The 33d Box Wagon came in a number of different liveries including those of LMS, SR, LNER and GWR. The important 30 Series made its entry with a Rolls Royce, a Daimler, a Vauxhall, a Breakdown lorry and an Ambulance finished in grey instead of white or cream. The 28 Series Delivery Vans appeared with an entirely new casting which would survive the War, but in the 1930s came in a wide variety of brightly coloured liveries including Atco Motor Mowers, Hartley's Jam, Crawford's Biscuits, Bisto, and Mackintosh's Toffee.

1936 saw the introduction of a small scale Austin Seven saloon, a M.G racing car and an M.G sports car. They all had tiny rubber wheels and tyres. An open Austin Seven was later added to

Some pre-war Dinky Toys with many post-war models.

From left to right. Top row: 39d Buick Viceroy, 39e Chrysler Royal, 39b Oldsmobile 6, 39a Packard Super 8, 30aGreen Chrysler 'Airflow' saloon, 30a (Pre-War) White Chrysler 'Airflow' saloon, 39f Studebaker State Commander. *Second row:* 34c Loudspeaker van, 280 red and blue Delivery vans, 151b 6-wheeled army lorries, 151 Royal Tank Corps Medium Tank Unit, 152b Reconnaisance car. *Third row:* 25f Market gardener's van, 25d green and red petrol lorries, 25c flat lorry and 25g trailer, 25a wagon (third type), later-lorries. *Fourth row:* 23m Thunderbolt, 23c Mercedes Benz, 23d silver and red (Pre-War) Auto Unions, 23a racing car, 35b midget racing car, 23p (M.G. 'R' type raced in 1935), 23e Speed of the Wind, 23b pre-war Hotchkiss, 23p Gardner's M.G. Record car, 33a Mechanical Horse and trailer, 30e Bedford breakdown van. *Bottom row:* 108 M.G. Midget (competition finish), 238 D Type Jaguar, 111 Triumph TR2 (competition finish), 110 Aston Martin DB3S (competition finish), 107 Sunbeam Alpine (competition finish), 163 Bristol 450 (competition finish), 23k Lago Talbot, 23g Cooper-Bristol racing car, 23j HWM, 35a Austin Seven saloon.

the range with a wire windscreen. There was also 23d, an Auto Union based on a model which was used either for record attempts or to compete with the Mercedes Benz team on the fast and banked Avus circuit.

In the next two years the range of 28 Series vans was increased even further and military vehicles were added including 151a, a tank which ran on metal chains, 151b which was an impressive six wheeled covered army lorry, and 152.b, a six wheeled reconnaissance car. The slender windscreen and side pillars of the reconnaissance car emphasised the extremely high quality of these early castings. The 23m Thunderbolt record car also joined the range, as did the 34b Post Office Van and the 36g London Taxi. The important 36 Series was issued in 1938, each equipped with tinplate figures. 36a was an Armstrong Siddeley saloon with a driver and a footman, 36b an two seater Bentley sports saloon with a driver and passenger, 36c a Humber Vogue with driver and footman, 36d a fastback saloon with driver and passenger, 36e a two seater sports Salmson and 36f a four seater sports Salmson both with drivers. They were 11d each or 5 shillings and six pence for the set.

Richard with his father's Dinky Toys, 1968.
Courtesy *Southern Daily Echo*

In the year before the War additions to the range included the 38 Series sports cars consisting of a Frazer Nash B.M.W, a Sunbeam Talbot, a Lagonda, an Alvis, a Triumph Dolomite and a S.S. Jaguar. The appropriately numbered 39 Series of American cars comprised a Packard, an Oldsmobile, a Lincoln Zephyr, a Chrysler and a Studebaker.

A pre-war Dinky Toy treasure

Many years after the War I was shown a large suitcase after it had been withdrawn from underneath a bed where it had remained undisturbed since 1939 when its owner had left home to join the RAF. Sadly, he was shot down in his Spitfire during the Battle of Britain and this was why the suitcase had been left untouched until that moment. Upon opening the case I discovered layer upon layer of pre-war Dinky Toys separated by sheets of pre-war newspapers. A number of cars were there with their little tinplate figures, the four Mechanical horse and covered trailers with their railway company logos, the later 28 Series vans with more varieties of logos than I thought had ever been made, and many others besides. It was as though every model in the Dinky Toy range had been bought and carefully stored away in that case under the bed. Sadly many of the models had become subject to metal fatigue, as is so often the case with pre-war Dinky Toys. Consequently they had become squashed with the weight of the models above them and crumbled to dust when touched.

Re-issued models.

From left to right. Front row: 30a Chrysler 'Airflow' saloon, 36e 2 seater British Salmson sports, 30d Vauxhall, 30c Daimler, 30b Rolls Royce *Second row:* 36c Humber Vogue saloon, 36d Rover, 36a Armstrong Siddeley, 36b Bentley, 36f 4 seater British Salmson sports, 36g London taxi with driver, Ambulance *Third row:* 38b Sunbeam Talbot sports, 38d Alvis sports tourer, 38a Frazer Nash BWM sports, 38e Armstrong Siddeley coupe, 38f Jaguar sports car, 38c Lagonda sports coupe *Back row:* 39c Lincoln Zephyr, 39f Studebaker State Commander, 39b Oldsmobile 6, 39a Packard Super 8, 39d Buick Viceroy, 39e Chrysler Royal.

All pre-war Dinky Toys are extremely rare today, partly because of the problem of metal fatigue, but also because, like so many mass produced toys, most eventually became lost or destroyed.

The models re-issued after the war

A small number of the pre-war Dinky Toys are said to have been released during the War years and certainly many more were produced in the years that followed immediately afterwards. They are easily distinguishable from the 1930s Dinky Toys because they had no tinplate figures and all the 30 and 36 Series models had black base plates and mudguards. The vans and lorries were devoid of any advertising logos, petrol tankers merely having PETROL printed in black along the sides, and the wheels of all the vehicles were ridged rather than smooth. For all that, it was a welcome return!

Entirely new models

The first entirely new model to emerge in 1946 was a military jeep. In 1947 the 25 Series lorries were given more substantial front bumpers and in the same year a Riley appeared, followed by the range of Super Dinky Toys modelled on Guy and Foden lorries. I was given a high-sided Foden

Post-war Dinky Toys and Supertoys from the Meccano Magazine in 1956.

THE MECCANO MAGAZINE

DINKY SUPERTOYS

No. 934
Leyland Octopus Wagon
Length 7⅝ in.　8/-

No. 965
Euclid Rear Dump Truck
Length 5⅜ in.　9/-

No. 918
Guy Van 'Ever Ready'
Length 5¼ in.　8/-

No. 923
Big Bedford Van 'Heinz'
Length 5⅜ in.　8/3

No. 955
Fire Engine
with Extending Ladder
Length 5½ in.　7/6

No. 963
Blaw Knox Heavy Tractor
Length 4⅝ in.　8/3

No. 982
Pullmore Car Transporter with Loading Ramp
Length (with Ramp) 18⅜ in.　17/6

MADE IN ENGLAND BY MECCANO LIMITED

Prices include Purchase Tax

lorry in brown and a Foden petrol tanker with a red cab and chassis and a plain grey tank. The petrol tanker was given to me as compensation for a painful visit to the dentist and I would gladly have repeated the visit for another similar model! In 1948 the all new Standard Vanguard appeared in fawn. My father had only just taken delivery of one of the very first Vanguards in egg shell blue and the Dinky Toy was a very accurate representation of it. The Dinky Toy range grew constantly in the years that followed. Notable were the new racing cars which were to be seen at Goodwood and Silverstone after the war. A No. 230 Lago Talbot, blue with yellow racing numbers, a No. 231 A6GCM Maserati, a No. 232 158 Romeo, developed from the Alfetta, a No. 233 2 litre Cooper- Bristol, a No. 234 Ferrari 500, strangely in blue and yellow of Argentina, and finally a No. 235 H.W.M.

A steady flow of new models was added to the range in the years that followed, so that miniature replicas could be bought in the toy shops of the cars that had first appeared in the London Motor Show at Earls Court the year before. An A90 Austin Atlantic was introduced in 1954, an M.G TF in 1955, a Triumph TR2 and a Ford Zephyr and an Aston Martin DB3S in 1956, the Sunbeam Alpine in 1957, and an Austin A30 in 1958 and a Ford Corsair in 1964. These are merely a few of what became a vast range for the collector to set his sights upon. As the number of models grew the numbering system of existing models had to be changed from two digits to three. Numbers from 100 to 200 were allotted to family saloons, 200 to 249 for racing and sports cars, 250 to 299 for buses, fire engines, police cars and other public service vehicles, 300 to 399 for farm vehicles and later cars, 400 to 499 for lorries, 500 to 599 for military vehicles, 700 to 799 for aircraft and 900 numbers for Super Dinky Toys.

When Corgi introduced their innovative range of cars with clear plastic windows in 1956 Dinky Toys were forced to up their game and so they followed suit the following year. Also in 1957 Dublo Dinky Toys appeared to complement Hornby Dublo trains, just as the earlier cars of 1:43 scale were intended to used in conjunction with Horny 0 gauge railways.

British Dinky Toys was taken over by Tri-ang in 1963 and the scale of the cars was increased from 1:43 to 1:35. Mattel joined the fray in 1967 with their Hot Wheels range and Dinky Toys competed with them with Speedwheels. Dinky Toys also introduced a range of vehicles which were associated with characters in children's television programmes such as Lady Penelope, Parsley the Lion, and Andy Pandy. Purists must have decried this development but Dinky Toys were, after all always intended for children!

Many of us look back with greatest affection to the Dinky Toys which belonged to our childhood. For me the earliest were the best, and their charm cannot be equalled by the most detailed scale models that have been made since.

16
CORGI TOYS

Mettoy

PHILIP ULLMANN AND ARTHUR KATZ established the Mettoy Company in Northampton and they issued their first lithographed tinplate models in 1934, the same year in which the first Dinky Toys appeared. At first the manufacture of Mettoy's products was subcontracted, being merely manufactured to Mettoy's design and, as was the case with Dinky Toys, all the resources of the Company had to be applied to the War effort from 1939 until 1945. It might be said that the War worked well for Mettoy inasmuch as, through the firm's greatly increased activities in producing mortar and shell carriers, it was able to move into a larger premises in Swansea in 1944. This resulted in Mettoy being more favourably placed when it resumed its production of metal toys.

As if to echo Frank Hornby's Modelled Miniatures, Mettoy launched what it called "Entirely New Miniature Numbers." One of its early products was a comparatively large scale racing car, being about eight inches long. It had realistic steering which was authentically operated by the steering wheel, a hand brake in the cockpit, and an exceptionally powerful clockwork motor. The car's body was made of heavy gauge metal but, disappointingly, it had stamped metal wheels and tyres which made it prone to wheel spin when run on a lino or wooden floor. I had a bright red example and my brother David's was white. They were both immensely strong but conformed to no other model's scale.

Mettoy became linked to Playcraft and the two companies later merged together. In 1954 they chose to give their new range of toy cars the name Corgi. This was because both their factories were situated in South Wales, making the Welsh Corgi dog an obvious candidate. Another reason for the name was its connection with the Queen's pet Corgis and this also made it a popular choice.

Corgi models

The first Corgi model cars, launched on 9 July 9 1956, were an Austin Cambridge, a Morris Cowley, a Riley Pathfinder, a Vauxhall Velox and a Hillman Husky. They were priced at 3 shillings and were all equipped with clear plastic windows, Glidamatic spring suspension, opening bonnets and jewelled headlights. Corgi set out from the beginning to take Dinky Toys on and certainly made their leading competitor look to its laurels and eventually to follow suit.

As a "Dinky" man, I was in two minds regarding this newcomer and thought that these innovations, while improving their play value, tended to make them less visually attractive as near scale models. Opening doors necessitated thickened pillars and the introduction of ugly interior hinges. In my view the "diamond jewelled" headlamps were less satisfactory than what had passed for headlamps before. However, there was no denying the fact that the new Corgis sold in large numbers and their success was in large measure due to the slogan that Corgis were "the ones with windows."

The Corgi Model Club was also established in 1956, encouraging its young customers to remain loyal to the brand in choosing additional models, and a regular news letter kept its members up to date with regard to forthcoming additions to the range.

In 1957 the first Corgi catalogue appeared and also the first gift set. Corgi advertised its products on television and its success was reinforced by the introduction of the popular Chipperfields Circus range in 1960.

Corgi Major gift set 27 Bedford Machinery Carrier and Priestman 'Cub' shovel, 1963.

The first Corgi Classics

In 1964 I was finally won over by Corgi through its first Corgi Classics. The range was limited and relatively expensive but its 1910 Daimler, finished in an attractive shade of red with beautifully cast yellow spoked wheels and its four plastic figures in period dress, was a must for any collection. This model was joined by a 1927 4.5 litre Bentley finished in a shade of green that was rather too pale for a Bentley but otherwise magnificent. There was a "World of Wooster" model with the plastic figures of Jeeves in the driving seat and Bertie Wooster standing alongside. There was also an interesting yellow 1910 Renault 12/16 Doctor's Coupe and two 1915 Model T Fords, one with its hood raised and unsuitably painted bright blue, the other with is hood lowered and in black. Top of the range was an ornate 12912 40/50 Rolls Royce Silver Ghost in silver with a finely modelled Silver Lady mascot. They all came in strong and attractively illustrated cardboard boxes and certainly broadened Corgi's appeal. Yet few at the time could have foreseen the huge importance that would later be attached to Corgi Classics. These early models marked the thirtieth anniversary of Mettoy.

Corgi classic 1910 Daimler, 1964.

James Bond's Aston Martin DB5

The popularity of Corgis' range of contemporary road vehicles, which was of course the firm's "bread and butter," took a great leap forward in 1965 with the introduction of James Bond's silver Aston Martin DB5. It was almost as full of gadgets as the car that it appeared in the film "Goldfinger" and it was an instant success. In addition to its opening doors, bonnet and boot, it had an ejection seat and machine guns which could be made to shoot out from its front. The success of the model, and that of the film, couldn't have done any harm to the sales of David Brown's Aston Martins either!

Largely due to the immense popularity of this single model, Mettoy received the Queen's Award to Industry the following year and also the Highest Standards Award of the National Association of Retailers.

The re-issued Aston Martin DB5.

Chitty Chitty Bang Bang

In 1966 Corgi did it again with its famous model of the children's favourite Chitty Chitty Bang Bang. I remember a friend of my parents in law calling at the rectory to give to our young son Richard one of these incredible models. It was a kind gesture that was typical of Gwyn but I wondered whether he couldn't resist going into a toy shop to get his hands on one of these fabulous models simply to examine it at close hand! Years later Corgi reissued Chitty Chitty Bang Bang and I bought one after seeing the new stage show in London. But why did they only supply it with the figure of Caractacus Potts and not those of Truly Scrumptious and the children?

In 1969 a fire caused extensive damage to Mettoy's warehouse in Swansea and this was a major set back for the firm as it was left with little to offer its retailers at a time when they were eagerly clamouring for more. Increased competition from Mattel also caused the Mettoy factory to be closed in Northampton but in 1974, from the "ashes of disaster grew the roses of success" in the form of an enlarged Corgi factory at Swansea.

The re-issued Chitty Chitty Bang Bang.

The State Landau

In 1977, the year of the Queen's Silver Jubilee, Corgi produced their State Landau complete with the realistic plastic figures of the Queen and Prince Philip and six horses in an attractive presentation box. Yet, in spite of this, the Company's future was in doubt and it was only saved by the formation of Corgi Toys Limited in 1984 which meant the end of Mettoy. Corgi Toys concentrated on the limited edition Corgi Classics which appealed to adult collectors rather than children all over the world. It was noticeable that the quality of the 1:50 scale range increased with each new model, and every casting was marketed with a variety of colourful liveries which led to increased sales. Ranges of Thornycroft and Bedford lorries, including some Bedfords with covered backs bearing the liveries of the four pre-British Railways companies were particularly good. These were followed by a range of Foden lorries and double decker Bristol K Utility, Guy Arab and Leyland buses. I remember Mr Potts of "The Railway Mart," Southbourne, remarking that the metal alone in these models was worth the price! Single decker half cab coaches accompanied them of similarly high quality, together with showman's engines and other steam vehicles. All were limited editions although the numbers produced saturated the demand so that most failed to achieve the inflated collectors' value that might otherwise have been expected. In spite of this prodigious output competition remained fierce and Corgi Toys Limited was bought by Mattel in 1989. Its base was moved from Swansea to Leicester and its models were made in China. It has to be admitted that this resulted in the quality improving yet more and in 1994 Corgi supplemented its 1:50 range of with the Original Omnibus range of 1:76 models which were ideal for 00 gauge model railways and provided competition for the extremely good Exclusive First Editions.

The Chipperfield Circus Range

To mark its 30th Anniversary of Corgi Classics Mettoy produced an entirely new range of Chipperfield Circus vehicles in 1994. It was extremely attractive and proved and an immediate success.

Chipperfield's Circus vehicles.

Corgi Classics Limited

In 1995 Corgi Classics Limited was formed and, separated from Mattel, had its premises were moved to Leicester. Bassett-Lowke was acquired by the new Company and its 0 gauge railway range subsequently increased. Corgi Collector centres were established, but in 1999 the Corgi was bought out by Zindhart in the United States providing the brand with a firm base on the other side of the Atlantic. Zindhart also acquired Lledo.

Most recently Corgi, including Bassett-Lowke and Lledo have been taken over by Hornby Hobbies who manufacture both Hornby trains and Scalextric cars. Hornby Hobbies continues to flourish so that all these and other famous British names are now in good hands.

Clockwise from top left: City of Oxford and wartime London Transport Guy Arab Utility buses; South Wales SEC Regal and Bedford OB coaches; Fowler B6 Crane Engine and Showman's locomotive; Corgi 'Legends of Speed' 1939 G.P. Mercedes Benz; Foden delivery truck and Leyland Tanker.

17
FROM LINES BROS
TO HORNBY HOBBIES

THE LINES FAMILY produced toys from the middle of the nineteenth century, and the brothers George and Joseph Lines founded their company G. & J. Lines in 1876. They soon employed a work force of 150 in their factory at Bagnidge Wells, Caledonian Road near Kings Cross Station in London. There they made wooden toys including many rocking horses for Gamages. In 1887 they patented the design of a hobby horse which they called the Jubilee Hobby Horse as it was the year of Queen Victoria's Golden Jubilee. Saddlers bought full-size wooden horses from Lines as models for their own products. Then, after George retired, Joseph moved to the Thistle Works, named after its thistle trade mark, in Down Lane, Tottenham where they built an entirely new factory. In addition to the factory itself they also owned extensive land at the site which included their own railway siding. G. & J. Lines closed in 1931 when Joseph Lines died.

Returning from the First World War in 1919, Joseph Lines' three sons, William, Arthur and Walter, having worked for their father from the time they had left school, established a new company, calling it Lines Brothers Limited. One of their company directors was Sir Ralph Freeman who had been involved in the design of the Sydney Harbour Bridge. The new company proved to be so successful that after two years the three brothers bought larger premises in Ormside Street off the old Kent Road and the London stores became important customers.

Their output growing all the while, the three Lines brothers moved into a new factory in Merton in 1924, near Wimbledon, with a staff of 533. They decided to call their products Tri-ang, as the three sides of the triangle which became their trade mark represented the three brothers, and their factory was known as the Tri-ang Works.

In 1931 Lines Brothers, with a staff of over a thousand, bought Hamleys and introduced two further important brand names, Pedigree, makers of dolls, and FROG makers of the model aircraft that "Flies Right Off the Ground". It became a public company in 1933.

Buying the Unique and Unity Cycle Company, Lines Brothers widened the range of their products still further, making tricycles, bicycles, scooters, pedal cars, doll's houses, and model boats, aircraft and road vehicles.

One of the more unusual Tri-ang products was the ice cream cart shown in the accompanying photograph. It has a wooden body with a metal chassis and wheels and the wording on its sides is strongly evocative of its period. The cardboard ice cream cartons, preserved from the same period, must be of considerable interest, as is the vehicle itself, to social historians.

In 1935 the Lines brothers launched the first series of tinplate clockwork Minic toy cars that were to be popular both before and after the War and which are described more fully below.

At the outbreak of the Second World War Lines Bros was forced to discontinue its toy production and in its place manufactured over the next six years one million machine guns and fourteen million magazines for our fighter aircraft, in addition to other munitions for the war. Their Merton

Very early Tri-ang ice cream cart.

Opposite: Pre-war Tri-ang Doll's Pram range and *(below)* pedal cars.

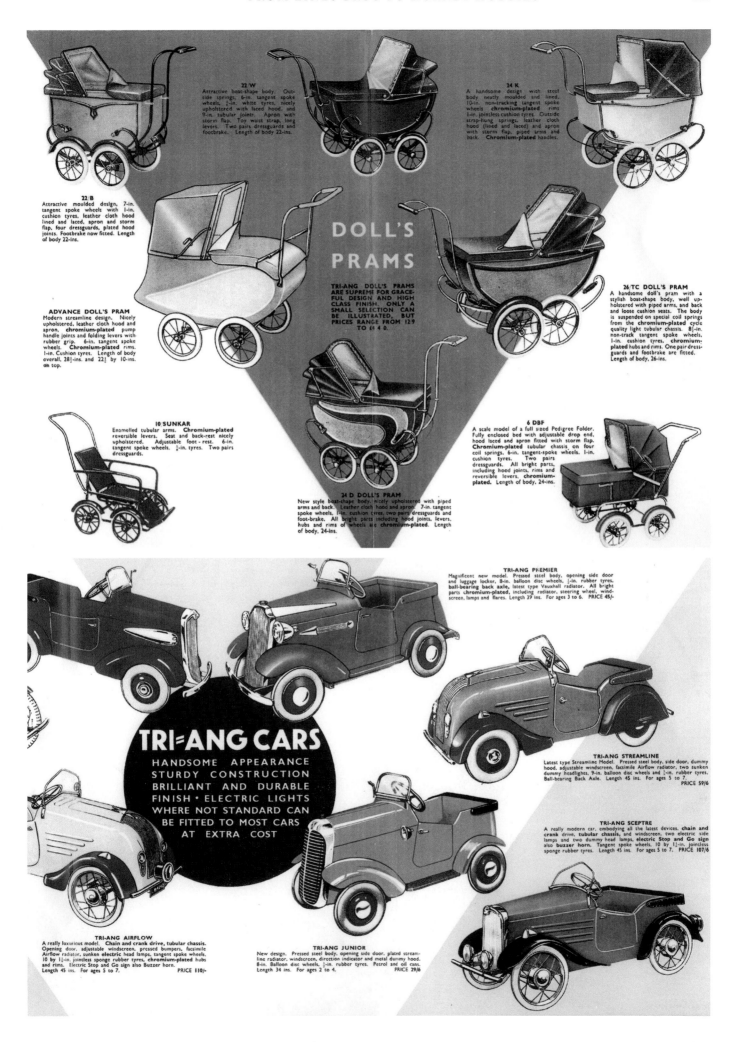

22/W
Attractive boat-shape body. Outside springs, 6-in. tangent spoke wheels, ⅞-in. white tyres, nicely upholstered with laced hood, and ⅞-in. tubular joints. Apron with storm flap. Toy waist strap, long levers. Two pairs dressguards and footbrake. Length of body 22-ins.

24 K
A handsome design with steel body neatly moulded and lined, 10-in. non-tracking tangent spoke wheels **chromium-plated** rims ⅞-in. jointless cushion tyres. Outside strap-hung springs, leather cloth hood (lined and laced) and apron with storm flap, piped arms and back. **Chromium-plated handles.**

22/B
Attractive moulded design, 7-in. tangent spoke wheels with 1-in. cushion tyres, leather cloth hood lined and laced, apron and storm flap, four dressguards, plated hood joints. Footbrake now fitted. Length of body 22-ins.

DOLL'S PRAMS

TRI-ANG DOLL'S PRAMS ARE SUPREME FOR GRACEFUL DESIGN AND HIGH CLASS FINISH. ONLY A SMALL SELECTION CAN BE ILLUSTRATED, BUT PRICES RANGE FROM 12/9 TO £4 4 0.

ADVANCE DOLL'S PRAM
Modern streamline design. Nicely upholstered, leather cloth hood and apron, **chromium-plated** pump handle joints and folding levers with rubber grip. 6-in. tangent spoke wheels. **Chromium-plated** rims. 1-in. Cushion tyres. Length of body overall, 28½-ins. and 22½ by 10-ins. on top.

26/TC DOLL'S PRAM
A handsome doll's pram with a stylish boat-shape body, well upholstered with piped arms, and back and loose cushion seats. The body is suspended on special coil springs from the chromium-plated cycle quality light tubular chassis. 8½-in. non-track tangent spoke wheels, 1-in. cushion tyres. **chromium**-plated hubs and rims. One pair dressguards and footbrake are fitted. Length of body, 26-ins.

10 SUNKAR
Enamelled tubular arms. **Chromium-plated** reversible levers. Seat and back-rest nicely upholstered. Adjustable foot-rest. 6-in. tangent spoke wheels. ⅝-in. tyres. Two pairs dressguards.

6 DBF
A scale model of a full sized Pedigree Folder. Fully enclosed bed with adjustable drop end, hood laced and apron fitted with storm flap. **Chromium-plated** tubular chassis on four coil springs. 6-in. tangent-spoke wheels. 1-in. cushion tyres. Two pairs dressguards. All bright parts, including hood joints, rims and reversible levers, **chromium-plated**. Length of body, 24-ins.

24 D DOLL'S PRAM
New style boat-shape body, nicely upholstered with piped arms and back. Leather cloth hood and apron. 7-in. tangent spoke wheels. 1-in. cushion tyres, two pairs dressguards and foot-brake. All bright parts including hood joints, levers, hubs and rims of wheels are **chromium-plated**. Length of body, 24-ins.

TRI-ANG PREMIER
Magnificent new model. Pressed steel body, opening side door and luggage locker, 8-in. balloon disc wheels, ⅞-in. rubber tyres, ball-bearing back axle, latest type Vauxhall radiator. All bright parts chromium-plated, including radiator, steering wheel, windscreen, lamps and flares. Length 39 ins. For ages 3 to 6. PRICE 45/-

TRI-ANG CARS

HANDSOME APPEARANCE STURDY CONSTRUCTION BRILLIANT AND DURABLE FINISH • ELECTRIC LIGHTS WHERE NOT STANDARD CAN BE FITTED TO MOST CARS AT EXTRA COST

TRI-ANG STREAMLINE
Latest type Streamline Model. Pressed steel body, side door, dummy hood, adjustable windscreen, facsimile Airflow radiator, two sunken dummy headlights, 9-in. balloon disc wheels and ⅞-in. rubber tyres. Ball-bearing Back Axle. Length 45 ins. For ages 5 to 7. PRICE 59/6

TRI-ANG SCEPTRE
A really modern car, embodying all the latest devices, **chain and crank drive, tubular chassis,** and windscreen, two electric side lamps and two dummy head lamps, **electric Stop and Go sign** also buzzer horn. Tangent spoke wheels, 10 by 1¼-in. jointless sponge rubber tyres. Length 45 ins. For ages 5 to 7. PRICE 107/6

TRI-ANG AIRFLOW
A really luxurious model. **Chain and crank drive, tubular chassis.** Opening door, adjustable windscreen, pressed bumpers, facsimile Airflow radiator, sunken **electric head lamps,** tangent spoke wheels, 10 by 1¼-in. jointless sponge rubber tyres, **chromium-plated** hubs and rims. Electric Stop and Go sign also Buzzer horn. Length 45 ins. For ages 5 to 7. PRICE 110/-

TRI-ANG JUNIOR
New design. Pressed steel body, opening side door, plated streamline radiator, windscreen, direction indicator and metal dummy hood. 8-in. Balloon disc wheels, ⅞-in. rubber tyres. Petrol and oil cans. Length 34 ins. For ages 2 to 4. PRICE 29/6

factory was damaged in an air raid in 1940 and King George VI visited it the following year.

Immediately after the war all the energies of the company were redirected once more to the peaceful object of making toys and Tri-ang opened new factories in Merthyr Tydfil in South Wales and Belfast in Northern Ireland. In 1946 Joy Toys Ltd was taken over both in England and New Zealand, and also W. Pearce which provided an important additional source of timber for the wooden toys at a time when that material was scarce. A further company was founded in Canada in 1947, and in 1951 Tri-ang bought a half share in Cyclops, an Australian toy maker. Importantly, in the same year Rovex Plastics Ltd was acquired through which Tri-ang made model railways and, at the same time, Rovex was moved to a factory in Margate.

Rovex and Tri-ang Hornby

Rovex, which was founded in 1946 by Alexander Venetzian, produced the "Princess Elizabeth" boxed 00 gauge electric train set for Marks & Spencer in a converted brewery in Richmond in 1950, just before its takeover by the Lines brothers. Then, having been absorbed by Tri-ang and

This page and opposite: From the *Tri-ang Hornby Book of Trains.*

R.450 Suburban Pantograph Motor Coach (above). A model of one of the New South Wales Government Railway Suburban trains that operate commuter services in Sydney, Australia. The model was designed in England and tooled up for production in Australia together with a centre car and non-powered unit. Operates from overhead catenary or from track power supply.

R.553 4-2-2 Caledonian Single. This famous old Locomotive, No. 123 which is still preserved, was an obvious choice to follow the "Lord of the Isles" (far left). Although both have a common style, they differ in practically every detail, leaving one to speculate about the different ideas of their original creators.

R.358 2-6-0 Old timer "Davy Crockett". Having made some provision for vintage enthusiasts in Britain, "Davy Crockett" was introduced in 1962 for 'Western' fans. The model is a free-lance design but incorporates the characteristic features of the period. Withdrawn from U.K. market in 1965.

R.357 A1A-A1A Brush Type 2 Diesel Electric. First model appeared in experimental blue B.R. livery (inset) in 1962. The following year, in line with B.R., green livery was adopted. In 1966 a different blue livery came in and this again was superseded in 1968 with yet another blue variation. It is a fine looking locomotive with above average performance.

25

moved to Margate, the Rovex branch of Tri-ang proceeded to acquire Pyramid Toys Ltd and to market 0-6-2 and 0-6-0 tank locomotives and wagons. By 1955 a range of ten locomotives was offered to the public and there was every indication that there were more on the way. Soon Tri-ang Railways were producing models in South Africa, Australia and New Zealand with a range that included models relating to those distant parts of the world. TT gauge railways were also added to the ambitious output.

The world-wide interests of Tri-ang Hornby were reflected in the *Tri-ang Hornby Book of Trains* in 1954 which contained illustrations of a Canadian Transcontinental Diesel locomotive and a Canadian Pacific steam model. In 1955 a 4-6-4 tank loco was introduced clearly intended for the South African, Indian, New Zealand and Australian markets. In 1956 a Diesel Switcher was made with the Canadians in mind and in 1958 the Australians, not to be left out, were offered a Transcontinental Diesel. In 1962 the 2-6-0 "Davy Crockett" joined the range and British vintage enthusiasts were not overlooked with the Caledonian Single, the Great Western "Lord of the Isles", and Stephenson's "Rocket", in each case accompanied by coaches which were appropriate to them.

R.55 Transcontinental Diesel. Introduced in 1954 for the Canadian market together with non-powered version R.57 to represent the back-to-back double heading so familiar across the Atlantic. The 'B' unit R.58 (inset) followed in 1956. The model has been made in Canadian Pacific and Santa Fe colours as well as the Canadian National illustrated.

R.55

R.54 4-6-2 Pacific (below). Also designed in 1954 for overseas markets. The model was based on a Canadian Pacific prototype and although withdrawn from sale in Britain in 1964, continues in production for export. Later models incorporate a front coupling, smoke generator, 'see-through' wheels and Magnadhesion.

R.54

R.56

R.56 4-6-4T. This was a compromise design for South Africa, India, New Zealand and Australia and introduced in 1955. The original was black (inset) but was changed to maroon livery in 1961 at the same time as a smoke generator was fitted. The locomotive was withdrawn at the end of 1962.

R.59

R.59 2-6-2T. A model of British Railways Class 3 Mixed Traffic Locomotive. First produced by Tri-ang in 1956 in lined out black livery, it was changed to green livery as run on the Western Region of B.R. in 1961. Temporarily withdrawn from production in 1966.

19

George and Richard Wrenn

George and Richard Wrenn began making 00 gauge track for model railways in the early 1950s at Lee Green in Blackheath. In 1955 they moved to Basildon in Essex and were soon responsible for a slot car racing system in addition to their expanding model railway range.

In 1960 Lines Bros, having been responsible for Tri-ang Railways through their subsidiary Rovex Scale Models, took over G. & R. Wrenn although George Wrenn kept a financial interest in his company. In 1964 George Wrenn took over Hornby Dublo and marked their models as Tri-ang Wrenn. The entire range of Tri-ang Wrenn locomotives was shown in the Tri-ang Hornby catalogue, the 4-6-0 "Devises Castle" and the 2-8-0 Class 8F still have diecast tender bodies while the rest were given plastic instead of tinplate tenders. Then, with the fall of Lines Bros in 1971, Wrenn took back complete control of his former company and called it Wrenn Railways. When I was planning an attempt on the world duration record for model trains I wrote to George Wrenn on the subject but he told me that he doubted the suitability of his locomotives for the task. George Wrenn retired in 1992 and consequently Wrenn locomotives acquired an added collector's value.

Getting acquainted with 00 gauge

The arrival of my son Richard in 1965 was the signal for me to get involved with 00 gauge model railways but I managed to wait for a couple of years before buying a Tri-ang Wrenn "Cardiff Castle", two Tri-ang Hornby GWR composite coaches, a brake third class coach with rails, controller and transformer. The plan was to store these until Richard was old enough to operate it all himself but it wasn't long before I put together a circle of track in the dining room table and put "Cardiff Castle" through its paces. This happened with increasing regularity until I decided the time had come to build a layout. It was the first of many, each one larger and more complex than the last, with buildings, trees, and road vehicles. Inevitably, as an inveterate collector, I assembled an extensive stud of locomotives and rolling stock while remaining fairly loyal to Hornby and Wrenn. In making a railway layout in the Rectory in Southampton I placed too much emphasis on the scenic effect, building a harbour with ships at a lower level with a bridge to take the trains across. It caused some difficulty in making the track absolutely level. As a result I built my next layout without any unnecessary complications! My eight year old daughter Wendy once offered to help me to construct this next layout but, wielding a chisel at the time, I told her that it was much too dangerous for her to use. Seconds later the tool slipped and I was on my way to Accident and Emergency to have to have a couple of stitches in my hand!

My brother David also had a succession of model railway layouts and an enormous collection railway stock. Whenever I stayed with him in Cornwall I took various locos to run on his layout and he would do the same when he stayed with me.

Model railways never really captured the interest of either of my sons, Richard and Michael, and perhaps that was one of the factors that prompted me to write this book.

The 1970 Tri-ang Hornby catalogue, which featured a Terence Cuneo painting on its cover, announced an entirely new model of the streamlined Princess Coronation Class 8P "Coronation" and an A3 LNER "Flying Scotsman" with glowing firebox, corridor tender and locomotive crew. Magadhesion was to be found throughout the range, improving the performance of all the models. The Battle of Britain Class Southern Railway Locomotive "Winston Churchill" and an LNER Class B12 also produced smoke from a heated capsule of oil. M7s in British Railways and Southern colours not only had glowing fireboxes and crew but also opening smoke box doors.

Hornby railways large scale live steam "Rocket".

Hornby Railways

Eventually the Tri-ang name was dropped and instead the products were known as Hornby Railways, being manufactured by Rovex Models and Hornby in the Westwood factory in Margate. In the 1970 catalogue there was a new Brush Type 4 Diesel Electric Locomotive and the 2-10-0 "Evening Star". Also new was a 2-6-0 Ivatt Class 2 Mixed Traffic locomotive and tender with glazed windows and vacuum pipes. The High Speed Train entered the ever growing range in Hornby's efforts to compete with Lima, Airfix and Palitoy.

After the sudden collapse of Lines Bros in 1971, due to a worldwide

Tri-ang *HORNBY* **LOCOMOTIVES**

R.864 4-6-2 PRINCESS CORONATION CLASS 8P LOCOMOTIVE "CORONATION" with tender and crew. Decorated in authentic L.M.S. livery, an alternative choice of 3 names is included with each locomotive. *(Available Summer 1970).*

R.855 4-6-2 CLASS A3 "FLYING SCOTSMAN" in L.N.E.R. livery with glowing firebox, corridor tender and locomotive crew.

Build up a specialised Locomotive Stud for the Passenger and Freight trains on your layout from the wide selection offered by Tri-ang Hornby and Tri-ang Wrenn.
You can select either from powerful modern diesel or electric locomotives, steam locomotives of British Railways or older steam locomotives in the liveries of the four famous Companies.

decline in the market, the great empire was broken up. Airfix bought Meccano, Dunbee Combex and Marx took over Rovex, and Tri-ang Pedigree went to Barclays.

From the 1970 Tri-ang Hornby catalogue.

Hornby Hobbies

In 1980 Hornby became subject to a management buyout and Hornby Hobbies Ltd became a public company in 1986. The new company purchased Dapol in 1996 and soon afterwards transferred the production of its models to China. The quality of its products just continued to improve.

Hornby Hobbies also embraces Scalextric, Airfix, Corgi and Bassett-Lowke and it was to Simon Kohler, Hornby Hobbies' Marketing Manager that I turned in 1988 in planning an attempt to establish new world records with Hornby trains and Scalextric cars to raise money for Christian Aid and the Church Urban Fund.

The record breaking "Lady Patricia"

I have recorded elsewhere in this book how we created a new World Record with a Scalextric Jaguar in 1989. On that occasion we failed in our attempts to establish a new record for model trains with a Hornby "Flying Scotsman" and a Hornby High Speed Train. The main reason for this was that, as the tracks had to be repeatedly cleaned with a cloth in the seconds that elapsed before the cars and trains passed by, very occasionally a thread from the cloth would break away unseen and become wedged in the joints between the rails. It would then be taken up by a wheel of the locomotive or one of its coaches and the additional drag caused the motor brushes to wear out prematurely. I believe that the problem was solved in subsequent record bids by welding the rails together so that they were continuous, but we stuck closely to the rules of the *Guinness Book of Records* as we saw them, which stated that only standard commercial products could be used in every aspect of the venture.

Battle of Britain class "Tangmere".

Merchant navy class "Brock-lebank Line".

Not to be defeated, we decided to make a second bid to break the non-stop duration record for model trains, and this time Jack Freeman built an even larger base board with four railway tracks in the study of my vicarage where I could more easily keep an eye on it. Peter Sparrow, the Bournemouth Hornby and Scalextric Agent, once again checked all the models over to make sure as far as possible that they were faultless and, once again, the four post-graduate apprentices from IBM in Hursley set up their computers to monitor the attempt. This time they arranged that a bell would alert me whenever one of the trains was failing to maintain a certain minimum speed. It meant that I sometimes had to come downstairs in the middle of the night to clean the track and turn the train's controller up. In spite of this the train would usually stop before the morning because of some underlying problem which could not be solved while it was in motion. There were plans to introduce locomotives with hardened brushes in the hope that these would be more durable. Had this proved to be the case a line of products would have been marketed by Hornby so that they would have become standard items in accordance with the rules. In the event we found that they didn't perform as well as the others and so they were not used.

For this second attempt on the record we had four locomotives each with six carriages from the Hornby range, and they were a British Railways "Evening Star", a Great Western "King Richard I", a "Lady Patricia" in British Railways blue, and a High Speed Train. On 14 February 1990 all the trains were assembled, and a group of Church members gathered in my study to watch Alan Cracknell, the Area Manager of British Rail, blow a whistle and wave a flag to start them off. All

"Lady Patricia" before the attempt on the record.

Jack Freeman and the author when 'Lady Patricia' was soon to establish a new world record.

four controllers were turned on while the mains switch was turned off. This meant that at the flick of one switch all the trains would start together. At 11 55am they were given a warming up lap to ensure that all was well before the actual start at 12 o'clock. Unfortunately "Lady Patricia" failed to start and there was no time to do more than to turn its controller up to provide greater power. The result was that, at 12 noon all four trains started but "Lady Patricia" rocketed off ahead of all the rest! The controller of the recalcitrant train was turned down to reduce its speed but, after precisely 29.58 minutes, according to IBM's recording apparatus, it stopped. It was immediately replaced by a black BR "Clevedon Court" and Peter Sparrow examined the blue model to ensure that all should be well when it was returned to the track. At 5 50pm the next day the BR "Lady Patricia" was able to begin a second attempt, pulling six Great Western coaches, after "King Richard I" had failed. It has to be said that a number of model trains were to be put through their paces over the next few weeks, mostly stopping with worn brushes, but on the evening of 22 March I deliberately took "King Richard I" off the track. It had been running for "only" three weeks and it enabled me to concentrate all my attention on "Lady Patricia" which was drawing close to breaking the existing record. Not long after this the motor in the tender of "Lady Patricia" began to make the most horrible noises, suggesting that it would not run much longer.

Earlier that day a camera crew from BBC Television had come to film the train as it circulated, with the intention of showing their footage the following day during the early evening news broadcast, if it was still running. It now seemed highly doubtful that they would be able to use the film. Drastic measures were necessary and so, after speeding the model up, I sprayed oil at the wheels of the tender with the intention of lubricating its motor. As I had anticipated, this resulted in the motor cutting out whenever the tender ran over a stretch of oil-soaked track and of course oil was constantly dropping from the motor on to the track. I spent literally hours late that evening and into the night continuously cleaning the track, constantly having to snatch my hand away so as not to connect with the flying train! Finally the motor was running continuously all the way round the track, sounding just as it should. In spite of this I kept the train running faster than normal throughout the night in case the motor cut out again and I only slowed the train to its normal speed early the next day. Somehow it continued through that day, apparently running quite normally, until a crowd gathered to watch it actually break the record. The BBC phoned up at 6 o'clock for confirmation that the train was still running and, as soon as the record had been achieved we all went into an adjoining room to celebrate the achievement and to watch "Lady Patricia" on television. The television newsreader commented that "the vicar was just chuffed."

We all forgot for a moment the train running alone in the study next door and, when I went in to check it, I heard the same horrible noise that I had worried me the previous evening. Of course I should have left well alone so that the train could struggle on until it finally expired, but I desperately attempted the radical remedy which had worked before. The result was that "Lady Patricia" stopped immediately and so that was that. When Peter Sparrow removed the tender body from its chassis he found that all the cogs of the main drive wheel had totally disappeared and it had become a completely smooth wheel! It was hardly surprising that it couldn't travel any further! Yet the record stood, and appeared with the Scalextric Jaguar in the 1990 *Guinness Book of Records*. "Lady Patricia" had run non stop for 867 hours 14 minutes and covered a distance of 640.89357 miles at an average speed of 0.739 miles per hour. James May please take note.

I presented Simon Kohler with "Lady Patricia" and the Scalextric Jaguar in special commemorative cases as I thought this was only right. Both were featured in the Hornby and Scalextric catalogues the following year.

Hornby Hobbies thrives as it continues to improve upon its excellent products which are now made in China. But where are all the young railway enthusiasts? The Hornby Thomas the Tank Engine range and Harry Potter's "Hogwarts Express" have drawn some youngsters to model railways from an early age and the preserved stream railways also help to stimulate their interest, but it is a tough battle against the small screen.

Minic

A wide range of tinplate Minic vehicles was offered both before and after the war. Being larger than diecast Dinky Toys, they didn't really fit in with other products. They were attractive and brightly coloured, and they had clockwork motors, but they were more toys than models. As with Dinky Toys, the post-war versions were slightly less attractive than the earlier models, lacking for example, the petrol cans that many pre-war models had on their running boards, and the rear luggage racks. The cars no longer had working head lamps and later post-war model lorries had forward control cabs instead of long bonnets. Favourites were a Green Line single decker bus and a red double decker London bus.

In the 1970s I was sent two large and unopened cartons packed tightly with boxed Minic vehicles which had been left at the back of the stock room of a shop and never been sold. I photographed two of the more unusual ones, a barrel lorry and an ambulance with the later forward control design.

Spot-On

In 1959 Lines Brothers decided to compete with Dinky and Corgi in the production of a range of die cast cars which they called Spot-On. They were manufactured in their Northern Ireland factory under the guidance of Murray Lines. They derived their name from being "spot on" 1:42 scale in contrast to their competitors who were rather more lax when it came to scale. The Spot-On scale of 1:42 was carried into their commercial vehicles as well, so they could be placed alongside the cars and looked right. The Spot-On vehicles met the two requirements of being sufficiently robust to be played with by children while also being accurate enough to satisfy the serious collector. The first Spot-On car was a Ford Zodiac and, like all those that followed, was made to a high standard and all the more attractive for being of a slightly larger scale. A Rolls Royce Silver Wraith was added to the range and a Phantom V, a large model which included plastic figures representing members of the Royal Family. Smaller models, built to the same scale included a Morris Minor 1000, Hillman Minx and Austin Devon. The Spot-On range was slightly more expensive than its competitors but was nevertheless good value. In 1964 Lines Brothers, having taken over Meccano and Dinky Toys, decided to kill off Spot-On in favour of the Dinky Toy brand. For years it seemed that the only lasting legacy of Spot-On was that Dinky Toys were now made to the scale of 1:42. I bought a Spot-On Morris Minor because that was the first car I had owned and many others must have bought that model for the same reason.

Recently the Spot-on name has been revived in a new range of model cars.

MINIC
2864 Rolls type Sedanca. With electric headlamps and battery. Length 5".
2858 Rolls type Sedanca. (Non-electric.)

MINIC
2852 Rolls type Tourer. (Non-electric.) Length 5".

MINIC 2854
Taxi. Length 4".

MINIC
2863 Daimler type Sedanca. With electric headlamps and battery. Length 5¼".
2859 Daimler type Sedanca. (Non-electric.)

MINIC
2853 Daimler type Tourer. (Non-electric.) Length 5¼".

2828 **MINIC** Open Touring Car. Length 4¾".

MINIC
2855 Caravan (non-electric) and Limousine. Overall Length 9½".
2833 Caravan (non-electric). Length 4½".

2829 **MINIC** Streamline Saloon. Length 5".

2832 **MINIC** Racing Car. Length 5½".

2867 **MINIC** Fire Engine with electric headlamps and battery. Length 6½".

2849 **MINIC** Dust Cart. Length 5¾".

2843 **MINIC** Luton Transport Van. Length 5¼".

2837 **MINIC** Tri-ang Transport Van. Length 5¼".

2836 **MINIC** Petrol Tank Lorry. Length 5¾".

2838 **MINIC** C. P. & Co. Van. Length 5¼".

2848 **MINIC** Tractor and Trailer with cases. Length 7¾".

2844 **MINIC** Lorry with cases. Length 5½".

2847 **MINIC** Mechanical Horse and Fuel Oil Trailer. Length 7".

2850 **MINIC** Steam Roller. Length 5¾".

2846 **MINIC** Mechanical Horse and Pantechnicon. Length 7½".

Page Twenty-eight

Pre-war Minic range.

Tri-ang Toys
The mark of Perfection

MINIC ALL TO SCALE CLOCKWORK TOYS

Almost every type of vehicle on the road represented; **some with electric lights.** Strongly constructed, and fitted with powerful, long-running mechanism, they will run anywhere, **even on the carpet.** Disc wheels, with rubber tyres. Each model is beautifully finished in a variety of colours, and packed singly in an attractive box. Various quantities according to type are packed in strong outer fibre cases for transit.

2845 **MINIC** Light Tank. Length 3½".

2822 **MINIC** Ford Royal Mail Van. Length 3½".

2821 **MINIC** Ford £100 Saloon. Length 3½".

2823 **MINIC** Ford Light Van. Length 3½".

2835 **MINIC** Tractor. Length 3".

2842 Vauxhall Cabriolet.

2841 Vauxhall Town Coupé.

2840 Vauxhall Tourer.

2851. Tourer with Passengers.

2824 **MINIC** Sports Saloon. Length 4¾".

2856 **MINIC** Mechanical Horse and Trailer with cases. Length 7½".

2830 **MINIC** Streamline Sports. Length 5".

2825 **MINIC** Limousine. Length 4¾".

2826 **MINIC** Cabriolet. Length 4¾".

2866 **MINIC** Double-deck 'Bus. Length 7½". Red or Green.

2827 **MINIC** Town Coupé. Length 4¾".

2831 **MINIC** Learner's Car. Length 4¾".

2834 **MINIC** Delivery Lorry. Length 5½".

2862 **MINIC** Single-deck 'Bus. Length 7½". Red or Green.

2839 **MINIC** Tip Lorry. Length 5½".

2861 **MINIC** Searchlight Lorry with electric searchlight and battery. Length 5½".

2865 **MINIC** Caravan Set (Tourer with passengers and Caravan with electric light). Overall length 9½".
2857 **MINIC** Caravan with electric light and battery. Length 4¼".

2860 **MINIC** Breakdown Lorry with Mechanical Crane. Length 5½".

Page Twenty-seven

Pre-war Tri-ang Minic range.

18
JACK ODELL

LESLIE SMITH AND RODNEY SMITH established a company to produce diecast models in 1947 together with Jack Odell who was a brilliant engineer and model maker. Although they shared the same surname the two Smiths were not related but formed the name of their company by using the first three letters of Leslie's Christian name and the last three letters of Rodney's. Their first toys were a tractor, a cement roller and a road roller and they measured up to eight inches long. The three then made a large model of the Coronation coach with the figures of the King George VI and Queen Elizabeth inside, which had an overall length, including the horses, of fourteen inches. At the time of the coronation of our present Queen they reissued the same model but with the figure of the King cut away at the lower portion of its legs. Look for the stumps if you see one of these! The large Lesney Coronation coach was naturally in great demand at the time in London and throughout the nation as a whole. A smaller edition was made with an overall length of only four inches. This was an even greater success and over a million were sold. Many years later the smaller coach became famous after one was shown on the children's television programme "Blue Peter" which had been sold in an auction for £50. It was a comparatively large amount of money at the time and caused a sensation as few had realised that toys might become valuable with age. As a result of this television exposure a great many more came to light but their owners soon discovered that, in consequence, their value had plummeted!

Matchbox Models

The first Matchbox model was produced when Jack Odell's daughter found that she wasn't allowed to take any toy into her school which was not small enough to put into a matchbox. In response to this rather arbitrary rule Jack made a miniature road roller in brass for her and this

Matchbox Superkings Grain Transporter K-3-E released 1980.

became the first of the 1–75 Matchbox models. The fact that their packaging had the appearance of being matchboxes undoubtedly added to their appeal but the quality of the casting in each case was exceptionally high and it was an attractive and popular series which remained unrivalled for many years.

Rodney Smith left Lesney in 1951, but Leslie Smith and Jack Odell stayed with the project and presided over its spiralling success.

Models of Yesteryear

It was Jack Odell who was primarily responsible for the introduction of the Models of Yesteryear and, using his unrivalled skills in producing precision diecast models of fine quality, he made the 1925 Allchin traction engine in 1955. It would remain one of the most popular of his models for all time but the following year he added to it the B Type London bus, the tram and the Sentinel steam lorry. The four were exhibited at the toy fair in Harrogate and were first marketed as Yesteryear models in 1957. The intention was to limit the range to fourteen so that every time a new model was introduced one of the existing models would be discontinued. It was to prove to be a good marketing strategy as it led to obsolete models rapidly acquiring a rarity value. However rules are made to be broken and Y15, the 1907 Rolls Royce Silver Ghost extended the range by one. The Rolls Royce was a good choice, being the car that has pride of place in the National Motor Museum at Beaulieu.

In 1960 the yellow 1904 Spyker, from the film "Genevieve" became Y16 to increase the range further still but, after this, Odell and Smith adhered to their rule so that, with the introduction of the 1905 Shand Mason horse-drawn fire engine, the Y4 Sentinel steam wagon was dropped. Other early Yesteryear models included a 1929 Le Mans Bentley, a 1908 Grand Prix Mercedes Benz, an 1862 American Santa Fe steam locomotive, and a Great Western Railway "Duke of Connaught". The first Yesteryear Gift Set was launched in 1961 and in 1966 Lesney won the Queen's Award to Industry. At the height of their success Lesney Smith and Jack Odell were both awarded the OBE and exported their products to 130 countries throughout the world.

The Second Series took the place of the First with, for example, the Y1 1911 Ford T, the Y3 1910 Benz limousine, and the Y9 1912 Simplex. Then the Third Series followed with such models as the Y2 1914 Prince Henry Vauxhall, and the Y4 1909 Opel Coupe. The 1930 Packard Victoria, designated Y15, represented a move to more recent models and there were those who saw that this might be the start of an unfortunate if inevitable trend. The most serious grievance that collectors were to have with Yesteryear models was that the same Ford and Talbot van castings were used again and again with different logos. It tended to make the shelves of Yesteryear models look frankly uninteresting, and some loyal collectors began to think that they were being taken for granted.

Eventually Lesney failed in the face of competition from the United States in the form of Mattel's "Hot Wheels" and changing economic conditions throughout the world. Jack Odell withdrew from the company in 1973 and in 1982 Matchbox Toys Ltd, as it had become, was taken over by the Universal Group.

Immediately before this the Y3 Ford Tanker was produced in green with the Zerolene logo. The intention had been to restrict this to being a free gift to all the retailers but a few examples found their way onto the shelves of some shops. I bought one in a Bournemouth shop for £5

Early Models of Yesteryear lined up to face forward

In front: Y1 Allichin traction engine; *First row:* Two Y2 Type B London buses and two Y3 trams; *Second row:* Y4 two horse drawn fire engines and two Y4 Sentinel lorries; *Third row:* Three Y9 Showman's engines; *Fourth row:* Y8 Bullnose Morris, Y5 Bentley, Y10 Mercedes Benz and two Y7 Jacob's Biscuit vans; *Fifth row:* Y13 Santa Fe locomotives, Y12 horse drawn bus, Y6 gravel and sand lorry; *Sixth row:* Y14 Duke of Connaught locomotive, Y13 Santa Fe locomotive.

Yesteryear Ford T vans.

Models of Yesteryear Grand Prix cars *From left to right:* two Y14 1935 ERAs, Y10 1957 Maserati 250F, Y16 1960 Ferrari Dino 246/V12.

while others were sold in Plymouth at the normal price. Soon the meagre supplies were exhausted and the model's price soared in the hands of collectors.

In the years that followed the Universal Group moved the production of Yesteryear models to Macau and the firm concentrated on limited editions. The Connoisseur Set came out in 1984 with model cars from the old Series Two range but it was not a great success. A 1919 Walker Electric Harrods van was made to be marketed only through that store, and in 1986 the Company became known as Universal Matchbox. A series of four racing cars was launched which comprised a 1932 Type 51 Bugatti, a 1935 ERA in black, a 1957 Maserati 250F, a 1960 Dino Ferrari and a 1930 4½ "Blower" Bentley. They were excellent models with their wire wheels well represented and it was a pity that the series was not extended further.

Other new models were revealed including a 1929 Leyland Titan bus and a 1922 Foden Steam Wagon, and in 1989 the Great Motor Cars of the Century Series, but the twelve models could only be obtained by mail order. It was a departure from the traditional practice and proved to be unpopular. When, in 1990, the Macau factory was replaced by a new one in China the policy was

Special edition YS-39 passenger coach and horses, 1820.

to make Yesteryear models with fewer liveries and shorter runs in an effort to win back the collectors. Tampo printing was introduced and the American cars were equipped with white wall tyres. In 1991 production runs were limited to 5000 and there was the return of the 4.5 litre 1930 Bentley, but now in blue, and the ERA racing car in the blue and yellow of Prince Bira's cars.

In 1992 the Universal Matchbox Company was taken over by Tyco Toys who offered a range of thirty models and the following year pledged to produce thirteen models a year. Matchbox Toys Ltd went out of business in June 1982 and the following September David Yeh of Universal Toys moved all the moulds to a new factory in Hong Kong to embark upon production there.

Lledo

Jack Odell, whose genius had been responsible for Lesney in its earlier years, established with Bert Russell a new company which he called Lledo, which he arrived at simply by reversing the letters of his surname. They bought a substantial proportion of the existing Lesney tooling and set up a factory in Enfield. Within a year a "Days Gone" range appeared in the shops, consisting of six models. The new name intentionally related to the earlier one and enthusiasts soon realised that, with Odell as the essential link, this was a series which was worth taking seriously.

The First Series of Lledo consisted of five horse-drawn vehicles and a Ford model T van. The horse drawn bus and fire engine were particularly good and there was also a milk float, a baker's van, and a horse drawn tram.

Collectors soon caught on to the presence of the Lledo range and bought into it. Unlike the First Series Yesteryear range the original Lledo models were to be continued for many years but other models were added to the range to keep the customers interested. As might have been expected the quality was good and they represented excellent value for money. In 1987 a very attractively presented boxed set of three was introduced to commemorate the 75th Anniversary of the Royal Flying Corps. It was the first of their products offered with a certificate in limited numbers. Next came two sets commemorating the 50th Anniversary of the Battle of Britain, one limited to 10,000 and other produced in unlimited numbers. In the early 1990s the Lledo range consisted of a series of impressive cars from the 20s and 30s.

Lledo horse drawn bus and Ford T van.

Vanguards

In 1993 Jack Odell introduced the Vanguard range. It was perfectly timed to capture what had become a period of nostalgia for many – the 50s and the 60s. A favourite Vanguard model was the Morris Minor Traveller with its wood-framed body. It was detailed, accurate and made precisely to the scale of 1:43. Equally important, the colour was absolutely perfect and this was to remain the case with all subsequent Vanguard models. By the end of the decade Lledo and Vanguard were producing over six million models a year and then, in November 1999, it was taken over by Corgi and later still by Hornby Hobbies so that Vanguards remain in production today.

To mark the 85th anniversary of Brooklands. Lledo Spirit of Brooklands. *Left to right:* 1931 Alfa Romeo, 1922 Aston Martin, 1923 Sunbeam, 1933 MG.

19
TRI-ANG MINIC
AND SCALEXTRIC

Minimodels

FRED FRANCIS ESTABLISHED A TOOL MAKING COMPANY in 1939 and when the war was over founded Minimodels Ltd in 1947 to produce Scalex clockwork-powered cars and boats. He was an enthusiastic sailor and so included miniature sailing boats in addition to motor boats in his Scalex range.

Minimodels clockwork powered racing cars, which first appeared in 1952, were designed to be raced around a miniature racing circuit and Francis went on to develop model cars powered by electricity from the mains supply like model electric trains but operated by individual hand controllers. They were presented to the Harrogate Toy Fair in 1957 with the name Scalextric and they were an immediate success. Such was the popularity of Scalextric that Minimodels sold out to Lines Bros, who of course traded under the name of Tri-ang, knowing that the larger company would be better able to cope with the growing orders. Lines asked their subsidiary company Rovex to take Scalextric on and one of the results of this was the adoption of plastic, instead of metal for the car bodies and instead of rubber for the track. The smaller scale Minimodels continued to be constructed in Havant until 1967, marketed as Tri-ang Minic.

Tri-ang Minic

Tri-ang Minic electric car racing sets and Tri-ang Minic road vehicles were attractively presented at the back of Tri-ang Hornby railway catalogues. They were built to the same scale as the Tri-ang Hornby railways and an extensive range included a Crime Patrol set, consisting of a white 3.4 litre Jaguar police car and a red E Type Jaguar, and a GT Championship Race set with both Ford and Ferrari GT cars. Also available were models of a Chevrolet Corvette Stingray, an Aston Martin DB6, a Humber Super Snipe, a breakdown lorry, a flat trailer, a caravan trailer and a double decker bus in red or green. In addition it was also possible to buy a trophy accessory set, an international circuit extension set, flags and fences, a mad motorist reversing hazard, a racing pit and a bungalow with garage. There was even a horse racing set complete with horses and riders attached to four-wheeled vehicles which enabled them to negotiate the jumps.

Scalextric

It was after the collapse of Lines Bros Ltd that Rovex-Tri-ang was taken over by Hornby Railways and the Scalextric and railway items were made in the factory in Margate previously owned by Lines Bros until the decision was taken to move the production to China.

The first Scalextric catalogue was produced in 1960 and it included a Lotus, a Vanwall, a Lister Jaguar and an Aston Martin. Each year thereafter new and improved models entered the range

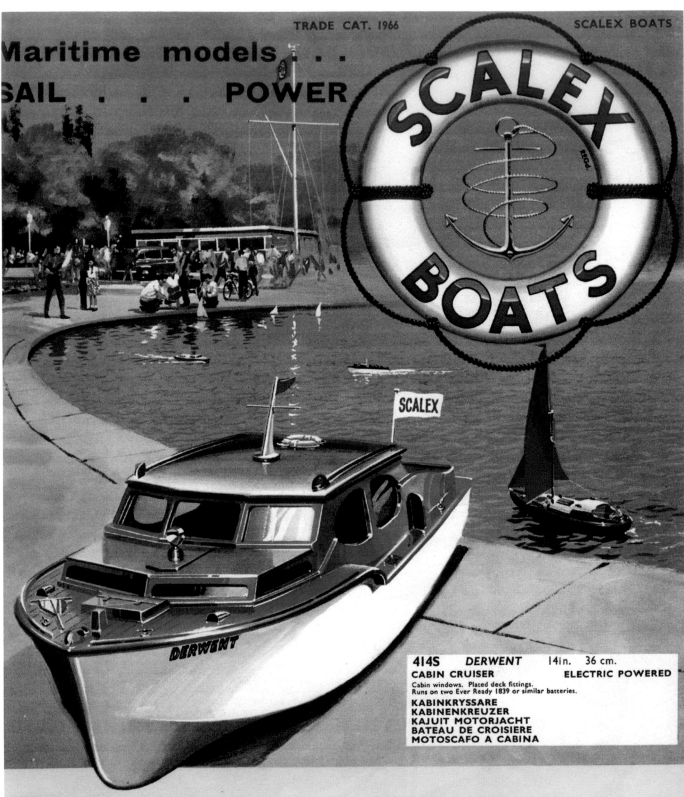

Scalex clockwork-powered
boats.

SCALEX yachts

BOAT STANDS

BS/1 STAND
Suitable for 7 in.—11 in. Boats

BS/2 STAND
Suitable for 12 in.—20 in. Boats

BS/3 STAND
Suitable for 8 in.—16 in. Yachts

H.216 *DIANA* 16 in. 41 cm.

OCEAN RACING YACHT
White hull. Red sails. Hinged mast.
Sailor man figure. Automatic rudder.

HAVSKAPPSEGLINGSJAKT
OZEAN-RENNYACHT
OCEAAN RACE-JACHT
VOILIER DE COURSE HAUTE MER
PANFILO DA REGATA OCEANICA

H.316 *SEAHAWK* 16 in. 41 cm.

OCEAN RACING YACHT DE LUXE
Black hull. Red sails. Plated deck fittings.
Two sailor men figures. Hinged mast. Automatic rudder.

HAVSKAPPSEGLINGSJAKT
OZEAN-RENNYACHT
OCEAAN RACE-JACHT
VOILIER DE COURSE HAUTE MER
PANFILO DA REGATA OCEANICA

Printed in England

Scalex yachts.

JJ 700
SEVEN JUMP SET
including THREE OPEN DITCH JUMPS

Jump Jockey
Electric Steeplechasing

Contents:

6 course straights	3 lap counters
10 course curves	1 winning post
3 horse, jockey and motor units	1 starting gate
4 course jumps	28 jump wings
3 open ditch jumps	3 prs. spare pick-ups
3 jump controllers	Full instructions

Size :
9' 0'' x 3' 9''   274 cm x 114 cm
Circuit length: 22' 0''   670 cm

Power Unit not included (*see page 31*)

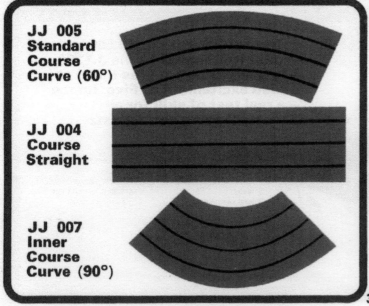

JJ 005
Standard
Course
Curve (60°)

JJ 004
Course
Straight

JJ 007
Inner
Course
Curve (90°)

JJ 012 LUCKY CHANCE
What's the odds ? — You fix them with
LUCKY CHANCE.
Complete with Counters

Jump Jockey
Electric Steeplechasing

1 2 3
4 5 6

LUCKY CHANCE

30

Mini horse racing set.

007 SET

★ **THE FABULOUS 007 CAR CHASE SET**

★ **007 ASTON MARTIN HAS EJECTOR SEAT AND WORKING BULLET PROOF SCREEN**

★ **SPECIAL MERCEDES WITH BUMPER ACTUATED CRASH ACTION**

★ **EXCITING TRACK SECTIONS:— 90° CROSSOVER, SKID CHICANE, EXTRA LONG CHICANE INCLUDES BEND**

1 Special 007 Aston Martin G.T.
1 Special Mercedes 190SL Sports
18' 8" (569 cm) of Track including:
4 Straight 'C'
8 Standard Curves
2 Converging Chicanes
1 Chicane Straight
1 Skid Chicane
4 Standard Curve Chicanes
1 Special Operating Straight
1 Right Angle Crossing
4 Straw Bales
8 Oil Drums
6 Banking Wedges
10 Marker Cones
2 Hand Throttles (A/265)

Drive the famous 007 Aston Martin G.T. and chase the underworld's Black Mercedes, catch it and ram its rear bumper, a spring will send it crashing off the Highway.

007 in the Aston Martin is well protected, if the Mercedes touches the rear bumper, a bullet-proof screen springs up behind the rear window.

The spy passenger is ejected through the Sunshine Roof after a rock in the road has been passed a number of times.

Care must be taken on the 90° Crossing and the various chicanes to avoid being rammed and crashed off the road by the other car.

(Power Unit not included, see Page 19).

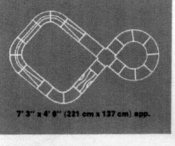

7' 3" x 4' 6" (221 cm x 137 cm) app.

HP/4 SPECIAL 007 CONVERSION SET. TO MAKE ANY **OTHER** SCALEXTRIC SET OPERATE 007 CARS
CONTENTS
1 007 Aston Martin
1 007 Mercedes 190SL
1 Special Operating Track
1 Straight 'D'

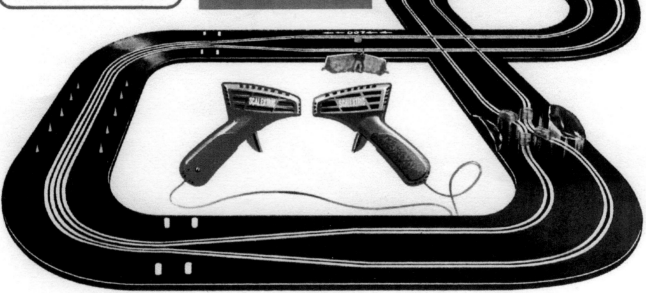

James Bond 007 Scalextric set.

SCALEXTRIC RACING MODELS

Four pages of fabulous Models for all types of racing. All those shown on this page can be used with any Scalextric Hand Throttle.

The Car colours given may, from time to time be changed to add even more variety to your stable of Cars.

C/3 JAVELIN SPECIAL Competition Car *(Available mid 1968)*
(Illustrated on page 2)

C/4 ELECTRA SPECIAL Competition Car *(Available mid 1968)*
(Illustrated on page 2)

C/60 'D' TYPE JAGUAR Competition (Green)

C/61 PORSCHE Competition (White)

C/75 MERCEDES 190SL Sports (White or Blue)

C/74 AUSTIN HEALEY 3000 Sports (Red or Green)

C/68 ASTON MARTIN G.T. with Sunshine Roof (Red or Green)

C/69 FERRARI G.T. (Red or Blue)

C/65 ALFA ROMEO 1933, Vintage Road Racing (Blue)

C/64 BENTLEY 1929, Vintage Road Racing (Green)

C/54 LOTUS Grand Prix (Yellow)

B 1 TYPHOON Combination (Red or Blue)

B 2 HURRICANE Combination (Green or Yellow)

Pages from the Scalextric catalogue.

C/10 SUPER JAVELIN (Navy Blue or Light Blue) *(Available mid 1968)*

C/11 SUPER ELECTRA (Orange or Red) *(Available mid 1968)*

C/88 COOPER Grand Prix (Red)

C/89 B.R.M. Grand Prix (Green)

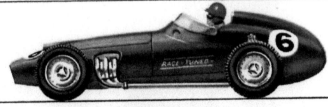

C/7 RALLY MINI-COOPER (Black or Green) *(Available mid 1968)*

C/32 MERCEDES 250 SL (Blue, White or Red) *(Available mid 1968)*

C/99 FIAT 600 (White or Red) *(Available mid 1968)*

C/90 FERRARI Grand Prix (Red)

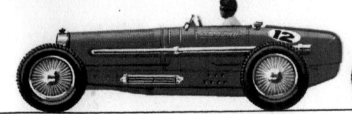

C/95 BUGATTI 1934 Vintage Grand Prix (Blue)

C/96 AUTO-UNION 1936 Vintage Grand Prix (White)

and those which were discontinued were sought by collectors. In 1962 an Aston Martin DBR and a Ferrari GT were equipped with lights, and in 1965 the popular Mini Cooper was introduced. In 1973 beautiful representations of the Tyrrell Ford and JPS Lotus entered the range. Scalextric has steadily advanced over the years with, for example, a succession of lap recorders each being an improvement on the last and, in recent years, with the introduction of digital control, enabling several cars to occupy the same track and also to swap tracks. The quality of the cars now compares with that of the better diecast models.

Tyrrell 019 of Jean Alesi.

Getting to grips with Scalextric

As was the case with 00 railways, I bought a Scalextric set long before Richard was old enough to get any use out of it, my excuse being that I could put it by for later on. It wasn't long before it came out of its box! It was a four-lane set, the largest in its range and, when my brother John and sister-in-law Elizabeth came over for the evening, John and I decided to assemble it all. The only way this could be accomplished was to place much of the furniture in the centre of the room and this meant that we couldn't know what was going on in the other half of the room and we coped with this by running the cars slowly over the unsighted section of track. It was of course an instant success and I had put a great many miles under my belt before Richard was old enough to get involved.

As with the trains, I took a number of Scalextric cars to Cornwall whenever I stayed with David and he in turn brought a number of his when he stayed with me.

Scalextric racing cars, from left to right: BRM, Ferrari Vanwall.

Airfix

In 1963 Airfix bought Model Road Racing Cars Ltd which was based in Boscombe, Bournemouth and introduced the Airfix Motor Racing slot car racing system in direct competition with Scalextric. A wide range of models was offered including a C Type Auto Union and a W125 Mercedes Benz and Vanwall. James Hunt's Championship winning McLaren was popular as was Niki Lauda's Grand Prix Ferrari. Airfix also produced plastic kits of such models as a Sunbeam Rapier and a Lotus Cortina which could be motorised and raced as slot cars. It was taken over by Palitoy of American General Mills in 1971 and finally by the people in Margate, who of course also owned Scalextric, in 2006.

The Jaguar's World Record

In 1989 I set out to establish World Records with a Scalextric car and a Hornby train to raise money for the Church Urban Fund. The plan was to hold a competition in which people would be asked to guess how long two cars and two trains would run without any outside interference before they finally stopped. Simon Kohler, the Marketing Manager of Hornby Hobbies, was very supportive in supplying models and equipment for the project together with prizes for the winners

Formual One Williams and Ferrari.

The World Championship Jaguar and the Castrol car.

Nigel Mansell's Williams Honda and Ayrton Senna's JPS Lotus.

Derek Bell's Le Mans winning Porsche.

and the Le Mans winner Johnny Dumfries gave me his Jaguar overalls as an additional prize. IBM devised a means by which the progress of the four models could be monitored and the exact time recorded when each finally stopped. The *Guinness Book of Records* were persuaded to allow a computer to be used in the place of human observers so that it wasn't necessary for people to be on hand twenty-four hours a day for several weeks. The Chase Manhattan Bank, now J.P. Morgan, met the cost of competition forms which were sent out to every diocese in the land. Jack Freeman, who was the church treasurer and also a model railway enthusiast, built the baseboard and laid the tracks in a large room within the church annexe. There were two outer railway tracks and two inner Scalextric circuits. Simon Kohler also sent me model grandstands, a railway station and other accessories to help complete the setting. The four competitors consisted of Johnny Dumfries' Le Mans winning Jaguar XJ8 and Nigel Mansell's Formula One Williams Honda, both of course by Scalextric, an LNER "Flying Scotsman" and High Speed Train both by Hornby. The rules demanded that each of the locomotives pulled six coaches and that they were all entirely standard models straight out of their boxes. The competition was launched at Jaguars in Coventry and I was photographed holding the Scalextric Jaguar while sitting on the bonnet of the car that actually won the 24 Hour Race at Le Mans.

On Tuesday 2 May 1989 John Curley, the BR Network South East Area Manager blew his whistle and all four models, which were operated by model railway controls, started at the touch of one switch at the mains. A large crowd had gathered in the hall next door where they could see what was happening by means of closed-circuit television. Eventually everyone had the opportunity to enter the room in groups to watch the scene before leaving to go home. Apart from regulating the speed of each of the models by means of the controls we could do no more than clean the track as they circulated and to spray small amounts of oil or WD40 at them as they came round. It was anticipated that the Scalextric cars would not last more than seventy-two hours so for the first three days and nights we had relays of four volunteers from the Church and the nearby Wentworth Milton Mount Boarding School to watch them for three hours at a time. The two trains stopped within three days but, to our surprise, the cars continued to circulate strongly. At nine o'clock on the first morning a radio car from BBC Radio Solent arrived to report live on air how things were proceeding. I estimated than the two cars must have driven the distance Bournemouth is from Ringwood by then and it hardly seemed possible. Radio Solent kept in touch with the project each week and on one occasion we had a visit from a crew from Sky News who filmed the cars clocking up their first three weeks. It seemed most likely that the Williams Honda would last longer than the Jaguar but one morning it was discovered that the head of the

The author with the Jaguar and Williams Honda on the inner Scalextric tracks.

plastic driver had somehow fallen off and this caused the car to lose contact with the power the next time it came round. A second Scalextric Jaguar in Castrol colours was put on the track to replace it but of course it had to start from scratch. Both Jaguars continued to circulate and someone would go to the room every three hours both day and night to clean the track and to check their speed. Then, at a late stage, those responsible for the *Guinness Book of Records* stipulated that one of the cars would have to keep going for five weeks if the record was to be recognised. In fact it managed to achieve this, running for 886 hours 44 minutes and 54 seconds. The car finally stopped not for any mechanical reason but because the lubrication had caused the tyres to swell and rub against the plastic wheel arches. The little car had covered an unbelievable distance of 1771.2 miles at an average speed of 2.03 miles per hour. The second Jaguar was still running strongly but a further two weeks would have had to elapse before it would have exceeded the record and the room was required for more conventional purposes. No one wanted to turn off the car's power because it just didn't seem fair! In the end I increased its speed minutely each day until it eventually left the track. This seemed to everyone to have been more acceptable! The success was duly recorded in the *Guinness Book of Records* and in the next year's Scalextric catalogue.

Soon afterwards I was contacted by the BBC in London who wanted to show the record-breaking Jaguar in the TV show "Record Breakers" with the late Roy Castle. A coach was arranged by the BBC to take many of those who had been directly involved to the television studio, and Hornby Hobbies set up a circuit on a baseboard for it to be filmed there. Fortunately I also sent an identical model as a reserve and it turned out that this was the one that was shown being out through its paces as the original car refused to start.

A further, and this time successful, attempt on the duration record for model trains to raise funds for Christian Aid is recorded earlier in this book.

The Jaguar on its way to a world record.

20
FILM AND TV RELATED TOYS

WHEN I BEGAN TO WRITE THIS BOOK it had already become clear to me that toys and models have had to compete with television and computer games for the attention of today's growing children, and it seems that it was in accepting the dictum that "if you can't beat them join them" the manufacturers seized upon every opportunity to produce toys and models based on popular films and television programmes.

I have already observed that one of Corgi's earliest and most spectacular successes was a model of James Bond's Aston Martin DB5 in "Goldfinger". To my mind the greatest of all the Bond films and the DB5 was the most memorable of all the Bond cars. Another Corgi model which was equally successful was the eponymous star of the film "Chitty Chitty Bang Bang." The two have earned a place in history, but there has been a plethora of film and TV related toys which have helped toy manufacturers to make profitable toys while enabling the makers of films and television programmes to generate additional revenue to meet their spiralling costs.

From Lesney's Disney series.

I remember when those who made television programmes for children first upped their game and embarked upon much more ambitious projects than had previously been attempted. In place of much loved but low-cost productions such as "Captain Pugwash" and "Ivor the Engine" in which the characters were two dimensional, rounded figures were made to move realistically by the technique known as Stop Frame Animation. Unlike Ivor, Thomas the Tank Engine ran upon the actual rails of an extensive model railway under its own power. Harry Potter's "Hogwarts Express" which followed some years later on the large screen was a real Great Western steam locomotive painted red. Hornby Hobbies was able to capitalise on both of them. Stop Frame Animation was used most successfully by Nick Parkes with his Wallace & Grommit films but the same technique had given rise to Trumpton, Camberwick Green, Chigley Postman Pat and many others. At first I wondered how the BBC could afford such expensive productions, in contrast, for example, to the low-budget "Picture Book" on "Watch with Mother", but then I learned that these

Basil Brush's car by Corgi.

Magic Roundabout figures by Corgi.

programmes were financed to a large extent by the commercial spin offs they generated. Porcelain buildings and figures could be purchased relating to Trumpton and Camberwick Green and these were followed by the figures of Postman Pat and his black and white cat. Corgi and Dinky Toys marketed models relating to Captain Scarlet and many others which are illustrated in this book. I wondered if, in some cases, the film makers may have thought first about the commercial potential of the spinoffs and only secondly about the content of their films! A glance at Ebay will reveal just how many film and TV related toys have been made. In addition to Hornby's Thomas the Tank Engine and "Hogwarts Express", Corgi produced a comprehensive range of models drawn from the films of James Bond, the Thunderbirds, Captain Scarlet, Wallace and Grommit, Only Fools and Horses, the A Team, The Italian Job, Starsky and Hutch, the Dukes of Hazard, Doctor Who, Red Dwarf, Star Trek, and Batman, in addition to Postman Pat, and the Little Red Tractor. All of these were reissued by Corgi to mark its 50th Anniversary and, from the Corgi Classics brochure of January to June 1995 can be seen models of Mr Bean's yellow Mini, Lovejoy's convertible Morris Minor, Spender's Ford Sierra Cosworth, and the Some mothers Do 'Ave 'Em pale blue Morris Minor. These were models for children to play with and enjoy but they are also highly collectable as they grow in nostalgic interest and rarity value. They may prove to be a channel through which many children who play with their toys will turn into adults who collect models.

Corgi's Mr Bean.

Thunderbirds Rescue pack by Matchbox.

The Transformers, in particular, has proved to be a marketing triumph in the realm of comics, films, television and toys. Hasbro, in recognising the value of the visual media, launched their range of Transformers models in conjunction with Marvel Comics and this was then followed by the television series and films.

It was in 1980 that the Japanese toy manufacturer Takara first produced a number of robots which transformed into vehicles and Hasbro acquired Takara so as to develop their idea and to produce their own range of models in 1984. Sunbow Productions produced the animated series for television and in 2007 Transformers: The Movie appeared, directed by Michael Bay and written by John Rogers, Robert Orci and Alex Kurtzman.

The association which exists between the toy and model manufacturers and the makers of films and television programmes will surely long continue to their mutual advantage.

Autobot Commander Optimus Prime.

Optimus Prime revealed.

TV and film related toys from Corgi.

R.351 'Thomas' the Tank Engine, No 1.
Length 4¹⁵/₁₆" 12.6 cms.

R.382 'Duck' GWR, No 8.
Length 4³/₄" 12.1 cms.

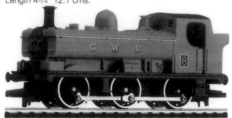

R.350 'Percy' the Small Engine, No 6.
Length 4¹/₄" 10.8 cms.

R.852 'James' the Red Engine, No 5.
Length 9¹/₁₆" 23 cms.

R.383 'Gordon' the Big Blue Engine, No 4.
Length 11¹/₈" 28.3 cms.

Thomas the Tank Engine
models by Hornby.

NEW	
R 2284	**'HOGWARTS CASTLE', CASTLE CLASS LOCOMOTIVE** Length 265mm *Available second quarter*

NEW	
R 4148 A/B	**HOGWARTS EXPRESS COMPOSITE COACH** Length 265mm *Available second quarter*

NEW	
R 4149 A/B	**HOGWARTS EXPRESS BRAKE COACH** Length 265mm *Available second quarter*

Harry Potter

Harry Potter's "Hogwarts
Express" from Hornby.

21
TOYS *ARE* FUN

TOYS ARE FUN – EVEN TODAY! James May proved this beyond doubt with his 3.4 mile Brooklands Scalextric track, his ten mile Hornby train set and his two storey Lego house.

Of course they no longer make tinplate cars, boats and trains like those that could be bought at Hamleys, Harrods and Gamages in Edwardian times. Hornby no longer make O gauge trains, but Bassett-Lowke and Ace do, and the latest 00 gauge Hornby trains are amazingly accurate models which offer the advantage of being digitalised. Meccano and Lego continue to produce construction sets, both Airfix and Revell still manufacture a wide range of plastic kits, and when it comes to diecast models there is Corgi, Spot-on Classix, Exclusive First Editions, Base Toys, Oxford, Hot Wheels, Britains, Minichamps, and CMC to name just a few!

So it may be asked, why I chose to call this book "When toys were fun?"

Well, my first reason was that, like many others, I recall the toys which belonged to my childhood and youth with a degree of fond nostalgia and, in addition, I have a particular affection for any models of cars, boats and trains which belong to a bygone age.

My second reason for casting the title in the past tense was the widespread belief that these days children prefer watching television and playing with computer games to enjoying their toys. Those options simply didn't exist when I was young and it has taken several decades for them to acquire the dominance they are said to have gained over the lives of so many children today. When my children were young "Disney Time" was a rare treat on Bank Holiday Monday afternoons whereas today there are dedicated digital channels which compete with each other in screening cartoons from morning to night seven days a week. Early computer games, with their

1:18 scale Ferrari 156 and C Type Autho Union by CMC.

grey and grainy images, were limited and temperamental whereas as today they are sharp, colourful and amazingly realistic. I'm not a Luddite and enjoy television and the occasional computer game as much as anyone, but I decided that it was time to investigate the extent to which toys have lost their appeal and the reasons why this may have happened.

One factor which had to be considered was the disappearance of so many toyshops from our town and city centres. Could this be entirely explained by the competition offered by the Internet and mail order companies, or was it also due to toys and models having simply fallen out of favour?

I called on a branch of "Toys R Us" to seek an answer to this and immediately discovered that there was certainly no shortage of toys! This great warehouse of a store was bursting with toys which were piled high and arranged in long aisles with short interlinking passages, reminding me of what Gamages must have been like years ago. Small children ran excitedly from one aisle to another, their eyes constantly lighting on something new, and there were traditional toys such as spinning tops, pedal cars, dolls and teddy bears as well as plastic toys of every description. But I asked the Manager why there didn't appear to be as many toys and models for older children as I might have expected and she looked around her and asked me in turn, "Where are all the older children?" She was of the opinion that older children were no longer interested in such things, and she supported the belief that they had turned to television programmes and computer games instead. To emphasise the point she added that even small children these days were only interested in drums if they were equipped with bells, whistles and above all had buttons to press, and she believed that the root cause of this was that parents no longer got down on their knees on the floor to play with their children because they found it easier to sit them down in front of a screen.

After this it was time to make my annual pre-Christmas pilgrimage to the London stores and I was pleased to see that both Harrods and Hamleys had a plentiful supply of toys and models to suit all ages. Hamleys had stacks of the latest electric train and slot car racing sets together with vast quantities of diecast models. Harrods, in addition to these, had some seriously expensive doll's houses, rocking horses and pedal cars which, although being several noughts above my modest budget were, as always, a delight to see.

Another notable toy shop that deserved my consideration was "Much Ado about Toys" in Stratford-upon-Avon which, being a traditional toyshop situated in the centre of the town, had a full range of toys and models from tinplate 0 gauge trains for the fathers to traditional toys for their youngest children.

Specialist model railway shops up and down the country, such as the Bournemouth Model Railway Centre, were well stocked with 00 gauge trains for the enthusiast and, just before Christmas in 2009, I was surprised to discover in Hobbycraft, a few miles from Bournemouth, detailed kits of a motor engine with moving parts which was marketed by Haynes and would surely be popular with any mechanically minded youngster.

Finally I went to the main branch of Marks & Spencer in Southampton where I again found models and kits for older children as well as toys for the very young. I noticed a large red sweet tin which conformed to the rudimentary shape a Brooklands racing car and it suggested to me the possibility that clockwork tinplate toys might one day return to the mainstream.

0 Gauge Bassett-Lowke Princess Helena Victoria.

It all indicated that, with so much on offer, there must still be many older children out there who are interested in the kind of toys and models which feature in this book.

The enthusiasm of adult collectors for toys and models continues unabated and the popularity of such magazines as *Model Collector, Diecast Collector, Railway Modeller* and *Model Rail* confirms this. There is so much on offer that collectors have to be disciplined in deciding upon a theme in order to keep their collections within bounds, and this may involve seeking discontinued models. It can still be done, as I found when I recently located some Crescent racing cars to photograph for this book on Ebay, and there is still immense satisfaction to be gained in tracking down the object of one's quest.

I remember an occasion in the 1960s when three young firemen called on me in Andover. They had come to buy a number of quite recently discontinued First and Second Series Yester-year models which happened to be surplus to my own collection. The models were neither rare nor expensive but it was as though these young men had stumbled upon treasure trove! They shared the spoils fairly among themselves and went away in high spirits. I wonder if they still have those Yesteryear models. The three of them may be grandfathers now and I wonder if their children and grandchildren are equally interested in their collections. Who knows, the day may come when my grandson's grandson will take a greater interest in that diecast model car!

1:18 scale Model of Captain Woolf Barnato's Bentley Speed Six by Minichamps.

144

Courtesy *Southern Daily Echo*